Quick & Easy Party Ideas For Kids

Craft, Game and Treat Ideas for Children's Birthdays & Holiday Parties

Linda Sadler

First Edition

Kansas City, Missouri

101 Quick & Easy Party Ideas For Kids

Craft, Game and Treat Ideas for Children's Birthdays and Holiday Parties

By Linda Sadler

Published By: Creative Kids Products
9825 NE 116th St
Kansas City, MO 64157-1106   U.S.A.

Printed in the United States of America

ISBN 0-9658527-3-3

Library Of Congress Control Number: 2005902638

Publisher's Cataloging-in-Publication information is available upon request.

DEDECATION and THANKS

To my mom, Marge Terflinger, for all of her
creative ideas and help, which made this book
possible. Her name should be on the front
cover with mine.

To my son Jason, who's creativity and skills
were invaluable in the design and production of
the cover and graphics included in this book.

To my husband Doug and son Kevin for their
never ending support.

Table Of Contents

Introduction..1
Helpful Suggestions 2

Craft and Party Favor Ideas

Introduction and Helpful Suggestions......................5
1. See-Thru Hearts...6
2. Woven Hearts 8
3. Sweetheart Arrows.......................................10
4. Stained Glass Hearts....................................12
5. Valentine People...15
6. Handprint Ducks..16
7. Chick Magnets...18
8. Bunny Signs...20
9. Fuzzy Bunnies 22
10. Chick Suckers..24
11. Bunny Suckers...25
12. Diving Birds...26
13. Easy Baskets...28
14. Fuzzy Flowers...30
15. Plastic Egg Chicks 31
16. Slinky Critters..32
17. Pastel Butterflies..34
18. Pastel Flowers..36
19. Tubular Bracelets..37
20. Balloon Yo-Yo's..38
21. Buggy Note Holders 39
22. Pencil Toppers...40
23. Balloon Walkers 42
24. Flower Pens & Pots 43
25. Funny Hairy's 44
26. Dandy Candy Airplanes...............................45
27. Silly "It's"..46
28. Patriotic Windsock......................................47
29. Smiley Play Dough 48
30. Fall Painted Pots 49

Craft and Party Favor Ideas (continued)

31. Leaf People..50
32. Scarecrow Treat Bag 52
33. Kitty Treats...54
34. Slime...56
35. Sugar Art 58
36. Pine Cone Bird Feeder 59
37. Cookies In A Jar...60
38. Shrinking Art 62
39. Reindeer Ornaments 65
40. Reindeer Treat Cups 66
41. Bead Candy Canes...67
42. Puzzle Piece Wreath 68
43. Pasta Tree Ornaments 70
44. Candy Cane Reindeer 73
45. Fuzzy Mice 74

Fun Party Games

Introduction and Helpful Suggestions......................77
46. Drawing Relay..78
47. Suck It Up Relay 79
48. Balloon Pop Relay...80
49. Scoop-It Up Relay...81
50. Back To Back Relay 82
51. Pass The Spider Race 83
52. Marshmallow Race..84
53. Magical Stick Relay 85
54. Pass The Teddy Bear 86
55. Siamese Twin Relay 87
56. Sucker Relay...89
57. Dress-Up Relay 90
58. Pass The Kiss Relay 91
59. Pass It Fast Relay 92
60. Balloon Platter Relay 93
61. Mysterious Relay...94
62. Almost A Kiss Relay 95
63. Soaking Wet Relay..96
64. Wheelbarrow Race 97
65. Dot Race 98

Fun Party Games (continued)

66. Buried Treasure Dig...99
67. Dice Twister.. 100
68. Bee Swat Race 102
69. Candy Drop Race... 103
70. Mummy Wrap Game 104
71. Party Scavenger Hunt 105
72. Balloon Stuff Game ....,........................... 106
73. Hit The Target Game 107
74. Suspended Apple Race 108
75. Party Bingo 110

Treat and Food Ideas

Introduction And Helpful Suggestions 115
76. Delightful Dippers 116
77. Spice Snack Mix 117
78. Bugs On A Log... 118
79. Toasted Bones.. 119
80. Toasted Snakes 120
81. Handy Treats.. 121
82. Take-Along Snacks....................................... 122
83. Cinnamon Tortillas 123
84. Taco Bar.. 124
85. Fruit Pizza 125
86. Fruit Kabobs 126
87. Cookie Cutter Sandwiches............................. 127
88. Mini Pizzas 128
89. Ice Cream Sundae Party................................ 129
90. Spring Cupcakes 130
91. Birthday Cookie 132
92. S'mores 133
93. A Real Sweet Train.. 134
94. Leprechaun Hats 135
95. Dirt Cups 136
96. Ooey Gooey Wormy Desert 137
97. Mini Ghost Cookies....................................... 138
98. Strawberry Smoothies.................................... 139
99. Stencil Brownies... 140
100. Snow Crunch 143
101. Snowman Cupcakes....................................... 144

List Of Figures

Figure 1   Clear Heart Pattern...7
Figure 2   Half Heart Pattern 9
Figure 3   Sweet Arrows Feathers Pattern...........................11
Figure 4   Stained Glass Heart Pattern 14
Figure 5   Duck Patterns...17
Figure 6   Chick Magnet Patterns...19
Figure 7   Bunny Patterns...21
Figure 8   Basket Pattern 29
Figure 9   Chick Patterns 32
Figure 10   Pencil Topper Patterns 41
Figure 11   Leaf Pattern..51
Figure 12   Cat Body Patterns 55
Figure 13   Cookie Recipe...61
Figure 14   Sample Shrinking Art Snowman Pattern..............63
Figure 15   Sample Shrinking Art Butterfly Pattern................64
Figure 16   Pasta Ornament Patterns 72
Figure 17   Fuzzy Mice Patterns..75
Figure 18   Dice Twister Game Board 101
Figure 19   How to suspend an apple by a string 109
Figure 20   Snowflake Stencils...141
Figure 21   Snowflake Stencils...142

Introduction

Hosting a party for your child is the perfect way to have a fun get-together with family, friends and neighbors. It takes a lot of planning and advance preparation to pull off a truly memorable party, so get the entire family involved and try to keep it simple.

101 Quick and Easy Party Ideas For Kids includes ideas that will help you create an extra special party favor or craft, serve fun and desirable treats, and play entertaining games. Use them as offered — or adapt them for your own special theme.

Each party idea is written in an easy-to-read format that includes the following:

Idea Introduction:
Suggests a way to use the idea at your party.

List Of Materials:
A detailed list of all materials needed to complete the project or activity is included with each idea. Most of the materials are easy to find either at home or at a local grocery, department or craft store.

How To Instructions:
Simple step-by-step directions are provided to help guide you through the entire activity. When helpful, I have included advance preparation steps. This allows you to be prepared, which is an important step to help make your party a success.

Read through the following ideas and have a great time planning your child's party. Remember to be creative and let your imagination run wild.

MOST OF ALL, MAKE IT FUN!

Helpful Suggestions

Planning The Party:

- Plan a party that will not only be fun for the children, but fun for you as well. If you try to take on more than you can handle, you will feel stressed and you probably won't have a good time. Remember, a party doesn't have to be a fancy affair. There are plenty of ideas in this book, so pick the ones that will work best with your theme or holiday. Plan the type of party that feels good to you and the children will have a wonderful time!

- Be sure to give yourself plenty of time to plan your child's party. Three weeks is usually enough time to get the invitations sent and supplies purchased.

- Pick and choose the ideas that are appropriate for the ages of the children that will be attending the party. Use the grade ranges that are included with each idea as a beginning guide. The best test is to have your child make the craft, treat or play the game before the party. Usually if they like the idea, then the children attending the party will too.

- When planning a party, timing is critical. Parties are a time of excitement and a child's attention span tends to be short. It is a good idea to include a few games, some treats and a fun craft that can be taken home as a party favor.

  If your party includes a large number of children, divide them up so that half are making their craft while the other half enjoy their treat. Save the games for last.

Planning The Crafts & Party Favors:

- Advance preparation is the secret to having a group of children complete a craft project within a short period of time. Most of the craft ideas in this book are designed to be assembled by children in a relatively short amount of time (15-30 minutes).

- Make at least one example of the craft. This will give the children a sample to look at and you will be better prepared to demonstrate the step-by-step instructions.

- The dimensions of this book did not allow all of the patterns to be drawn to scale. Use a copy machine, scanner or grid paper to enlarge the drawings as necessary.

Planning The Games:

- Plan more games than you think you will need in case some of them turn out to be too difficult or do not appeal to your guests. If the children are having fun with a game, let them continue to play. If they appear to be bored, move on to the next game.

- Try to alternate quiet and active games. By doing this, you maintain a desirable energy level among the children and prevent them from getting overly excited or bored.

- Make sure you have plenty of room to play the games that you have chosen. Since children tend to be clumsy, make sure that anything fragile or sharp is well out of the way. Do this throughout your house, not just in the game area.

Game Prizes:

- You will need to decide whether or not to offer prizes. If you do award prizes, try to make sure that everyone receives one. Simple, inexpensive prizes such as rings, pencils, erasers and stickers work well for children. Consider nonmaterial prizes, such as going first in the next game or receiving a round of applause from the group.

  Older children enjoy dividing into teams and keeping track of the points earned. When the games are complete, each member of each team should receive a prize.

Planning The Treats:

- Consider the ages of your guests when deciding on the amount of food you will need. Young children are often too excited to bother with food at parties. Make portions small and serve seconds if needed.

- To help prevent spills, make sure all of the children are seated before their drinks are poured. It is also a good idea to fill their cups only half full.

- Do not serve beverages that stain, such as grape juice.

- Serve beverages that come in cartons with straws inserted into the carton-top holes. They come in a variety of flavors, are almost spill-proof, and they save the trouble and expense of cups. (Remind the children not to squeeze the box.)

Safety Reminders:

- Carefully monitor all activities involving children and scissors. For young children, we strongly suggest using safety scissors for all of the craft projects.

- Hot glue guns are recommended for a number of the craft projects. It is very important that ADULTS ONLY use the hot glue guns. Always exercise extreme caution when using a glue gun.

- When using balloons, make sure that children play with only the inflated and intact balloons. Immediately dispose of all balloons that break. Swallowed or inhaled balloons or balloon pieces present a serious suffocation threat.

Craft and Party Favor Ideas

No party would be complete without the traditional take-home bag of candy and cheap toys, right? Why not replace it with a 'make and take' craft project? Most are simple, easy-to-make and require materials that are readily available. These craft projects will encourage children to be creative, use their imaginations, and give them a sense of accomplishment. Most of all, they will have a great time!

Helpful Suggestions:

- Make sure you follow the advance preparation tips. This is the secret to having a group of children complete a craft project within a short period of time. Most of these crafts are designed so the children are simply 'assembling' the craft project. Older children can often do their own cutting and painting. You be the judge.
- Pick crafts that are age appropriate.
- Make at least one example of the craft. Do this with your child. This will give the children at the party a sample to look at and you will be better prepared to help them make the craft.
- The dimensions of this book did not allow all of the patterns to be drawn to scale. When specified, use a copy machine, scanner or grid paper to enlarge the patterns.
- Use a hot glue gun in place of regular glue. Things will stay together better and dry faster. But supervise children at all times.
- Place all of the pieces for each craft in plastic bags (one for each child) and simply hand them out when it is time to make the craft.
- Allow plenty of time for the children to complete their fun take-home party favor.

See-Thru Heart   Grades K-5

Hang these colorful hearts in the window to brighten up the last few months of winter.

Supply List

Paper—heavy red or pink
Ribbon or Yarn—red or white
Clear Contact Paper—shelf liner
Vinyl Suction Cup—optional
Confetti—heart shaped

Paper Punch, Scissors, Tracing Paper, Cardboard, Pencil

Advance Preparations:

▶ Cut the red or pink paper into 5"x 5" squares. Do the same with the contact paper.
▶ Cut the string into 15-inch lengths.
▶ With the tracing paper, copy the pattern in Figure 1 and cut out. Copy this pattern onto a piece of cardboard and cut out. (Or make your own pattern.)
▶ Using the cardboard heart as a pattern, trace the hearts onto the heavy paper. (Let older children design their own hearts.)

How To Make Them:

1. Cut out the heart shape by following the drawn lines.
2. Carefully peel the backing off of one piece of contact paper and place sticky-side up on the table.
3. Place the cut-out heart directly in the middle of the sticky paper.
4. Fill the center of the heart with confetti.
5. Carefully peel the backing off the remaining piece of contact paper and place on top of the heart (match the corners as close a possible).
6. Press around the edges to seal.

7. Cut out the heart.
8. With the hole punch, cut one hole in the top center of the paper heart.
9. Thread the piece of ribbon or yarn through the punched hole and tie into a knot. If you are using suction cups, thread the other end of the string through the hole in the suction cup and tie into a knot.

Variation:

- Instead of using the heart pattern, make your own pattern for the holiday or special occasion that you are celebrating. These might include: shamrocks, eggs, flowers, leaves, pumpkins, Christmas trees, stars, bells....etc.
- Use confetti that is appropriate for your party's theme.

Figure 1
Clear Heart Pattern

Woven Hearts   Grades 2-5

These paper hearts look great hanging from a door knob or kitchen cabinet. Be sure to write a special Valentine message on the top corner of the heart.

Supply List

Construction Paper—white
    and red
Ribbon or Yarn—red or white
Marker—red or black

**Glue, Paper Punch, Scissors,
Tracing Paper, Cardboard,
Pencil**

Advance Preparations:

▶ Using the tracing paper, copy the patterns in Figure 2 and cut out. Copy this pattern onto the piece of cardboard and cut out.
▶ Cut the white and red construction paper into 3"x 4½" pieces.
▶ Using the cardboard pattern, line up the flat side of the pattern with the 3-inch side of the rectange. Trace the rest of the pattern onto the white piece of paper.
▶ Next, mark off each inch along the 3-inch side that is not curved. Using these marks, lightly draw two lines that are about 3¼-inch long, as shown in Figure 2.
▶ Cut the ribbon or yarn into 15-inch pieces.

How To Make Them:

1. Take the white piece of paper, with the pattern drawn on it, and place on top of a red piece of paper. You are getting ready to cut both pieces of paper at the same time.
2. Round off one end of each rectangle along the drawn lines. Next, cut along the two long lines.
3. Lay the shapes on top of each other to form a heart shape.

4. Now comes the tricky part. Take one of the top strips and weave it under, over, then under the strips on the underneath piece. Weave the next strip the opposite way by weaving it over, under, then over the underneath piece. Weave the third strip like the first strip.
5. Line up the edges and place a few drops of glue across the strips on the back of the heart to hold them in place.
6. With a marker, write a special valentine message on the front of the valentine.
7. With the hole punch, make a hole in the top center of the heart.
8. Thread the piece of yarn or ribbon through the hole and tie into a knot.

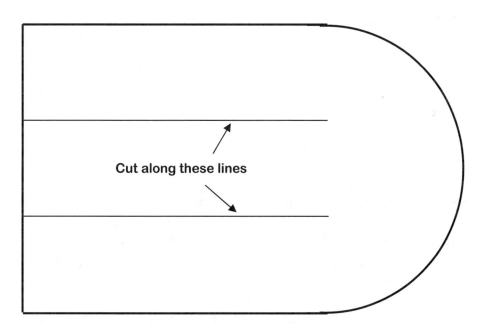

Cut along these lines

Figure 2: Half Heart Pattern

IDEA #3 Sweetheart Arrows Grades 1-5

There will be no problem hitting the target of your special Valentine with this sweet craft idea. Their sweet tooth.

Supply List

Wooden Skewers—6-inch
Candy Bars—small
Miniature Candy Bars
Large Candy Hearts
Red Tissue Paper
White Tissue Paper

Scissors, Tape, Ruler

Advance Preparations:

▶ Cut the red and white tissue paper into 4-inch squares.
▶ Place a white square on top of a red square.
▶ Put a piece of tape along one side to hold them together.
▶ Make the arrow's 'feathers' by cutting along the dashed lines as shown in Figure 3.

How To Make Them:

1. Carefully push the skewer through the middle of the candy bars (leave wrappers on).
2. The last piece of candy to go on the skewer should be the heart. Put it on sideways to make the 'arrowhead'.
3. To make the 'feather', roll the tissue paper around the skewer.
4. Use tape to fasten it to the stick and to keep it from unrolling.

Suggestion:

• Use candy bars with loose fitting wrappers and candy with soft (not solid) centers. Small packages of gum will also work.

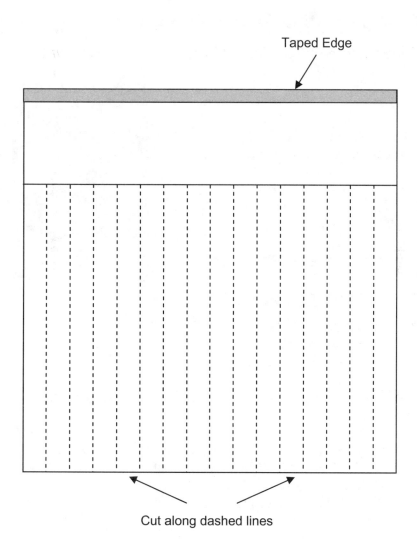

Figure 3
Sweetheart Arrows Feathers Pattern

IDEA #4 **Stained Glass Hearts** Grades 3-5

This is an easy way to make real looking stained glass out of paper.

> ### Supply List
> **Construction Paper**—black
> **Tissue Paper**—red and white
> ___
> **Scissors, Cardboard, White Lead Pencil, X-Acto or Utility Knife, Carbon Paper, Glue, Pencil, Tape**

Advance Preparations:

▶ Enlarge Figure 4 so it fits on a 6" x 9" piece of paper.

▶ With the carbon paper, copy the pattern onto the piece of cardboard. With the knife, carefully cut out the pieces that are not black.

▶ Cut the pieces of black construction paper in half. Each sheet should be approximately 6" x 9".

▶ Using the cardboard pattern and the white lead pencil, trace the stained glass pattern onto each piece of black construction paper.

▶ Draw an X in the middle of each piece that will be cut out (not black on the pattern).

▶ Cut the red and white tissue paper into 6" x 9" pieces.

▶ Make a sample by following the directions below.

How To Make Them:

1. Take the black construction paper and carefully cut out the center shapes (the pieces marked with an X) by following the white lines.

2. Tape the black sheet to a table with two pieces of tape.

3. Place the white tissue paper over the black sheet and tape down. You should be able to see the black paper through the tissue paper.

4. Decide which sections you want to be white, and draw around the outside edge of them with a pencil. Be sure to draw the shape a little larger than the hole.

5. Continue drawing around all the shapes that you want to be white.
6. Remove the white tissue paper and cut out the outlined shapes.
7. Repeat steps 3-6 with the red tissue paper.
8. You should now have a cut out shape for each hole.
9. Next, carefully put a small amount of glue all around the edges of one hole. Place the matching piece of tissue paper over the hole to glue in place. Smooth out any wrinkles with you finger.
10. Continue this process until all of the holes are covered with tissue paper.

Did You Know?

- The average adult heart beats 60 to 100 times a minute.

- A heart will beat more than 2.5 billion times during an average lifetime.

Figure 4
Stained Glass Heart Pattern

IDEA #5

Valentine People

Grades 3-5

These cute little guys will bring a smile to anyone that is lucky enough to receive one.

Supply List

Red Construction Paper
White Construction Paper
Paper
Cardboard
Black Felt Tip Marker

Glue, Pencil, Scissors, Ruler

Advance Preparations:

▶ Cut a 3½" square out of a piece of paper. Fold in half and cut out a heart. Repeat with a 1½" piece of paper. Copy these patterns onto a piece of cardboard and cut out.

▶ Using the cardboard hearts as a pattern, trace the heart shapes onto the red construction paper. Each child will need 1 large and 4 small hearts. You can let the children cut out their own hearts if there's enough time.

▶ Cut red and white construction paper into 1/2" x 12" strips. (4 per child) Use a paper cutter if you have access to one.

▶ Cut additional red and white construction paper into 3/4" x 12" strips. (4 per child)

How To Make Them:

1. Glue 1 white and 1 red 1/2" strip together at right angles—like the letter L.
2. Fold the bottom strip over the top strip (accordion style) and repeat until the strips end. Glue the last fold.
3. Repeat steps 1-2 with the other six pieces of paper.
4. Glue the small hearts to one end of each folded strip.
5. Glue the 1/2-inch strips to the large heart for the arms.
6. Glue the 3/4-inch strips to the large heart for the legs.
7. Draw a face on the large heart with a black marker or use stickers.

IDEA #6 Handprint Duck Grades K-5

These handy ducks are quick and easy to make any time of the year.

Supply List

Yellow Craft Foam
Orange Craft Foam
Wiggly Eyes—10 mm
Magnetic Tape
Small Stickers

Glue, Scissors, Pen, Tracing Paper, Cardboard

Advance Preparations:

▶ Cut yellow craft foam into pieces that are large enough for 2 handprints. Use your child's hands as an example.

▶ Using the tracing paper, copy the shapes in Figure 5 and cut out. Copy these patterns onto the piece of cardboard and cut out.

▶ Using the cardboard pattern, trace the Body pattern onto the yellow craft foam. Each child will need 1 body piece. Cut apart.

▶ With the cardboard pattern, trace the Beak and Feet patterns onto a piece of orange craft foam. Cut apart. Each child will need 2 Feet and 1 Beak.

▶ Cut the Magnetic Tape into 1-inch pieces.

▶ NOTE: For young children: cut out the body pieces for them. This way they just have to glue the pieces together.

How To Make Them:

1. On the large piece of yellow craft foam, use a pen to carefully trace around the child's two hands. Cut out.

2. Cut out the other body parts that are on the pieces of yellow and orange craft foam. (1 body, 1 beak and 2 feet)

3. Using the picture as a guide, glue the cut-out hands to the back of the body.
4. Again, using the picture as the guide, glue the feet, beak and wiggly eyes onto the body.
5. Decorate as desired with small stickers.
6. Peel the back off the magnet tape and attach to the back of your duck.

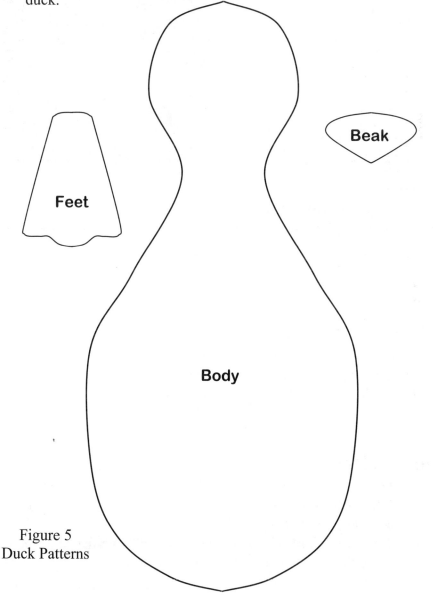

Figure 5
Duck Patterns

Chick Magnet

IDEA #7

Grades K-5

Boys and Girls alike will enjoy making these colorful magnets, which can decorate a refrigerator all year round.

Supply List

Craft Foam-2 colors
Feathers
Wiggly Eyes-12 mm
Chenille Stems
Stickers & Glitter Pens
Magnetic Tape

Scissors, Pencil, Cardboard, Tracing Paper, Glue (hot glue works best)

Advance Preparations:

▶ Using the tracing paper, copy the shapes in Figure 6 and cut out. Copy these patterns onto the piece of cardboard and cut out.

▶ Using the cardboard pattern, trace the Body pattern onto one color of craft foam. Each child will need 1 body piece. Cut apart.

▶ With the cardboard pattern, trace the Beak and Feet patterns onto the second color of craft foam. Cut apart. Each child will need 2 Feet and 1 Beak.

▶ Cut the Chenille stems in half (6-inches long).

▶ Cut the Magnetic Tape into 1½-inch pieces.

▶ NOTE: For young children: cut out the body pieces for them. This way they just have to glue the pieces together.

How To Make Them:

1. Cut the body parts out of the craft foam. (1 body, 1 beak and 2 feet)
2. Using the picture as a guide, glue the eyes and beak in place.
3. Turn over the body.
4. Take the chenille stems and wrap loosely around a pencil to make the legs. Glue to the body.

5. Glue a small single feather to top of the body.
6. Again, using the picture as the guide, glue two feathers to each side of the body for the chick's wings.
7. Turn back over and glue the feet to the end of the legs (top side).
8. Decorate as desired with glitter pens and small stickers.
9. Peel the back off the magnet tape and attach to the back of your chick.

Suggestion:

- To help keep the parts glued on this chicks, and to save drying time, you might want to use a low temperature hot glue gun. Set up a gluing station and have the children put the pieces of their chick in place while an adult applies a small amount of hot glue. The beak and eyes can be put on with regular glue, but we have found the hot glue works best for the rest of the body parts. Be careful not to touch the hot glue or the tip of the hot glue gun. Always have an adult apply the hot glue!

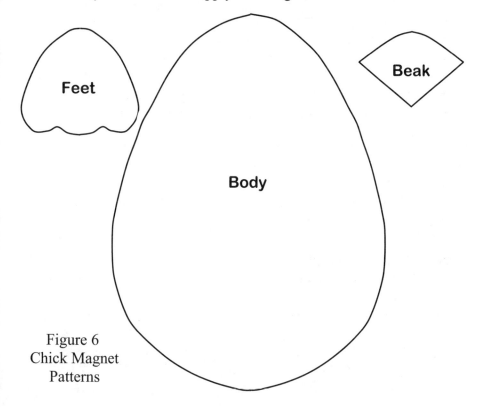

Figure 6
Chick Magnet
Patterns

(IDEA #8) # **Bunny Signs**   **Grades K-3**

Hop to it and personalize this cute bunny with your name, or a special message like Happy Easter.

Supply List

White Craft Foam
Pink Craft Foam
Styrofoam Cup—8 oz
Styrofoam Ball—2-inch
Wiggly Eyes—10 mm
Black Fabric Paint
Ribbon—narrow ¼-inch

Scissors, Pencil, Cardboard, Tracing Paper, Knife, Glue (hot glue works best)

Advance Preparations:

▶ Using the tracing paper, copy the shapes in Figure 7 and cut out. Copy these patterns onto the piece of cardboard and cut out.

▶ Using the cardboard pattern, trace the Ear and Feet patterns onto the white craft foam. Each child will need 2 Ear and 2 Feet pieces. Cut apart.

▶ With the cardboard pattern, trace the Inside Ear and Nose patterns onto the pink craft foam. Cut apart. Each child will need 2 Inside Ear pieces and 1 Nose.

▶ With a knife, carefully cut a small slice off the Styrofoam ball so it sits flat and doesn't roll around.

▶ NOTE: <u>For young children</u>: cut out the body pieces for them. This way they just have to glue the pieces together. Also, paint the mouth and whiskers on the Styrofoam head for them.

How To Make Them:

1. Cut the body parts out of the craft foam. (2 white ears, 2 pink ears, 1 nose and 2 feet)

2. Turn the cup upside down and glue the Styrofoam ball to the bottom of the cup.

3. Glue the pink ear to the middle of a white ear. Try to line up the bottoms. Repeat with the second ear pieces.
4. Using the picture as a guide, glue the ears to the lower back part of the Styrofoam ball head.
5. Glue the pink nose to the center of the head.
6. Glue the 2 wiggly eyes above the nose. Use the picture as a guide.
7. Glue the 2 feet to the lower edge of the cup.
8. Tie the ribbon into a bow and glue to the front of the cup.
9. When the glue has dried, carefully lay the bunny on it's back and use the fabric paint to add a mouth and whiskers to it's face.
10. Write your name or a special message on the front of your bunny. You can use fabric paint or a colored permanent marker.

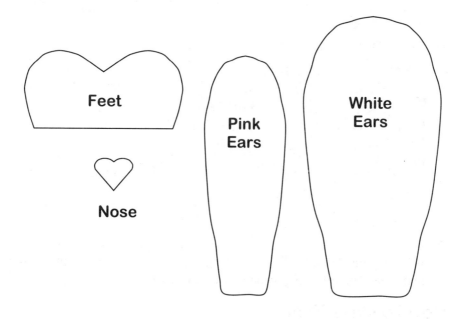

Figure 7
Bunny Patterns

Fuzzy Bunnies   Grades K-4

These cute little bunnies will make you smile! They also make great additions to any Easter basket.

Supply List

White Pompoms—2-inch (1),
   1½-inch (1), ¾-inch (5),
   ½-inch (2)
Pink Pompom—¼-inch (1)
White Felt
Pink Felt
Wiggly Eyes—10 mm
Ribbon—¼-inch

Tacky Glue, Scissors, Pencil,
Tracing Paper, Cardboard

Advance Preparations:

▶ Using the tracing paper, copy ear shapes below and cut out. Copy these patterns onto the piece of cardboard and cut out.
▶ Using the cardboard pattern, trace the Large Ear pattern onto the white felt and the Inner Ear pattern onto the pink felt. Cut apart. Each child will need 2 Large and 2 Inner Ears pieces.
▶ Cut the ribbon into 8-inch lengths.
▶ NOTE: For young children: cut out the ear pieces for them. This way they just have to glue the pieces together.

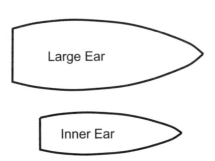

Large Ear

Inner Ear

How To Make Them:

1. Glue the pink inner ears to the middle of the white ears. Make sure the bottoms line-up.
2. For the nose, glue the two ½-inch pompoms together.
3. Using the picture as a guide, begin assembling the bunny by gluing the 1½-inch pompom head to the top of the 2-inch pompom body.
4. Glue four ¾-inch pompoms to the body for the legs and arms.
5. Glue the last ¾-inch pompom to the back of the body for the tail.
6. Glue the two nose pompoms to the lower part of the head and then glue the ¼-inch pink pompom to the middle of the nose.
7. Glue the wiggly eyes to the head.
8. Glue the ears to the back of the head. Make sure they stick well above the bunnies head.
9. Tie the ribbon into a bow and glue to the front of the bunny.

Variation:

- Try other colors of pompoms and ear shapes to make other animals (such as a brown bear or a black and white dog).

Did You Know?

- Rabbits have about 28 teeth.

- It takes one month for a female rabbit to have a litter of babies, and they can have as many as eight babies at one time.

Chick Suckers   Grades 1-3

IDEA #10

Turn a simple sucker into a fun spring or Easter treat.

Supply List

Large Suckers
Yellow Tissue Paper
Orange Yarn
Orange Felt
Yellow Felt

Black Felt Tip Marker, Glue, Scissors

Advance Preparations:
▶ Cut the yellow tissue paper into 8"x 8" squares.
▶ Cut the yarn into 10-inch lengths.
▶ Cut the orange felt like Pattern 1 for the beak.
▶ Cut the yellow felt like Pattern 2 for the chick's top feathers.

Pattern 1

Pattern 2

How To Make Them:
1. Hold the sucker upright and place the tissue paper over the top of it. The sucker should be in the middle of the tissue paper.
2. Wrap the tissue paper down over the sucker.
3. Take the yarn and tie a bow right below the candy ball. Trim the ends if they are too long.
4. With the black marker, draw two solid eyes.
5. Bend the orange felt beak in half and glue below the eyes.
6. Glue the yellow felt top feather to the top of the chick's head.

Suggestion:
• If the candy wrapper is dark and showing through the tissue paper, cut a piece of facial tissue into a 6"x 6" square and place over the sucker before the tissue paper.

Bunny Suckers   Grades 1-3

These look cute in a basket with the Chick Suckers.

Supply List

Large Suckers
Purple Tissue Paper
Dark Purple Ribbon
Purple Thread

Scissors, Black Fine Tip Marker, Glue

Advance Preparations:

► Cut the purple tissue paper into 8"x 8" squares.
► Stack two tissue paper squares on top of each other and cut a small hole in the middle of the papers. It should be large enough for the sucker stick to go through.
► Cut the ribbon into 10-inch lengths.
► Cut the thread into 10-inch lengths.

How To Make Them:

1. Poke the sucker stick through the hole in the middle of two pieces of tissue paper.
2. Gather the tissue paper above the candy ball and twist.
3. Take the thread and tie a knot above the candy ball. A partner is really helpful for this step.
4. Fan out the tissue paper and cut a V in the center of it.
5. Gather 1/2 of the tissue paper and twist to form an ear. Repeat for the second ear. Place a little glue on the paper ends to hold them down.
6. With the black marker, draw the eyes, nose and mouth on your bunny.
7. Take the ribbon and tie a bow right below the candy ball. Trim the ends if they are too long.

(IDEA #12) **Diving Birds**   Grades K-5

Put these Birds on a long string and watch the children have a great time racing each other.

Supply List

Plastic Cups—16 oz
Yellow Paper
Wiggly Eyes—10 mm
Feathers—multiple colors
Plastic Straws
String

Scissors, Glue, Tape, Tracing Paper, Cardboard, Razor Blade or Utility Knife

Advance Preparations:

▶ Using the tracing paper, copy the beak pattern below and cut out. Copy this pattern onto the piece of cardboard and cut out.

▶ Using the cardboard pattern, trace the beak pattern onto the yellow paper.

▶ Cut the straws in half.

▶ Cut the string into 15-inch lengths.

▶ With the cup standing upright on the table , measure about 1/3 up on the cup, and with a razor blade or utility knife, <u>very carefully</u> cut a 1½ to 2-inch slit horizontally (left to right) in the side of the cup. This is where the wing feathers will go. Repeat on the opposite side of the cup for the second wing. **Only an adult should do this step!**

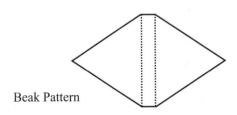

Beak Pattern

How To Make Them:

1. Pick out six feathers.
2. Place the bottom of 3 feathers together and spread the tops out to look like wings.
3. Place a 1½-inch piece of tape across the bottom of the grouped feathers.
4. Carefully turn the feathers over and place another 1½-inch piece of tape over the other piece of tape.
5. Repeat steps 2-4 with the other 3 feathers.
6. Find the slits in the side of the cup, press the cup in just above the slit, and place taped end of one of the wings through the slit. You might have to trim the tape if it won't fit through the slit.
7. Repeat step 6 for the other wing.
8. Lay the cup on it's side and glue the wiggly eyes on the bottom of the cup. They should be centered between the two wings.
9. Make the beak by folding the yellow paper at the bottom of the two triangles (along the dashed lines). Use the picture as a guide.
10. Glue the flat part of the beak to the bottom of the cup below the eyes.
11. Tape the straw to the top of the bird, between the two wings. Make sure the end of the straw is over the lip or top of the cup.
12. Thread a piece of string through the straw.
13. Have a second person hold the end of the string that is on the bird's beak side.
14. Move the bird to the other end of string.
15. Have the second person sit on the floor or hold their end of the string on the floor.
16. Have the children raise their birds over their heads. Let go and the birds will race down the string.
17. Have the second person hold two strings at a time and the children can race each other.

Easy Baskets

IDEA #13

Grades K-6

Make these for Easter, May Day, or any other time of the year. Add candy and flowers to make them extra special.

Supply List

Yellow Poster Board
Stickers
Green Easter Grass
Foam—1-inch thick

Scissors, Pencil, Ruler, Pen,
Knife, Glue or Glue Stick

Advance Preparations:

▶ For the basket's handle, cut a 9-inch by ¾-inch strip out of the poster board.

▶ Cut an 8-inch square out of the poster board. Refer to Figure 8 for help marking the cuts and folds for the basket.

▶ Draw a line 2-inches in on all four sides.

▶ To make folding the poster board easier, go over each of these lines 3 or 4 times with a pen. Make sure you press down very hard.

▶ Cut along the four lines that are labeled "cut" in Figure 8.

▶ With a seriated knife, cut the foam into 4-inch squares.

How To Make Them:

1. Using Figure 8 for reference, fold along all the dashed lines.

2. Starting with one corner, bend flap 'A' up, bend the adjacent flap 'B' up, and pull flap 'A' behind flap 'B'. Apply a small amount of glue to the back side of flap 'A' and glue to 'B'. Hold in place until the two flaps are stuck together.

3. Repeat step 2 with the other three corners to make the bottom of the basket.

4. Glue the handle strip to the inside of two opposite sides of the basket. Hold in place until stuck together.
5. Decorate the outside of the basket with stickers.
6. Place the square piece of foam inside the basket.
7. Cover the foam with Easter grass.
8. You're done! Now add candy, some Fuzzy Flowers (page 30), Chick Suckers (page 24), Bunny Suckers (page 25) or Fuzzy Bunnies (page 22) to make it really special.

Suggestion:

- Instead of glue, use double sided tape.

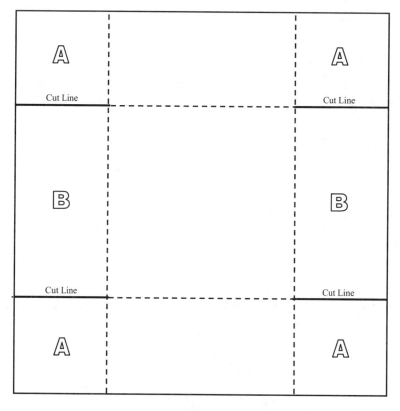

Figure 8
Basket Pattern

Fuzzy Flowers   Grades K-5

Make a bouquet of these easy flowers and then put them in a vase or the Easy Basket (page 28) for safe keeping.

Supply List

Chenille Stems—green & flower colors
Bump Chenille Stems— green & flower colors
Pompoms—1-inch & ½-inch

Scissors, Glue (hot glue works best)

Advance Preparations:

▶ For the flower stems, cut the green chenille in half (6-inches).
▶ For the leaves, cut the green bump chenille into 2 bump pieces.
▶ For the petals, cut the bump chenille into single bump pieces. You can also use regular chenille and cut one stem into four pieces.

NOTE: This craft is fun because there is no specific way to make these flowers. Bend and glue the chenille to make different types of flowers. A couple examples are given at the bottom of this page.

How To Make Them:

1. Take the petal pieces and bend each petal so the ends meet.
2. Glue the petals to the backside of a pompom.
3. Glue the flower stem to the back of the flower.
4. Wrap the center of the leaf pieces around the stem so there is one leaf on each side of the stem and they stay in place.

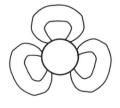

IDEA #15 **Plastic Egg Chicks**   Grades K-3

Put some jelly beans in this easy little craft for a special take-home treat.

Supply List

Plastic Egg—yellow
Felt—orange and yellow
Wiggly Eyes—8 mm
Curtain Ring—1-inch white

Scissors, Glue, Tracing Paper, Cardboard

Advance Preparations:

▶ Using the tracing paper, copy the shapes in Figure 9 and cut out. Copy these patterns onto the piece of cardboard and cut out.
▶ Using the cardboard pattern, trace the beak and feet patterns onto the orange felt and the wing, tail and hair patterns on the yellow felt.
▶ NOTE: <u>For young children</u>: cut out all the pieces for them. This way they just have to glue the pieces together.

How To Make Them:

1. Cut all the pieces out of the orange and yellow felt.
2. Bend the beak piece in half along the dotted line and glue to the middle of the egg, just below the middle joint.
3. Using the picture as a guide, glue the wiggly eyes, wings, feet, hair and tail to the egg. If you are putting candy in the egg, make sure you do not glue the wings over the middle joint.
4. Glue the ring to the bottom of the feet to help the chick stand up.

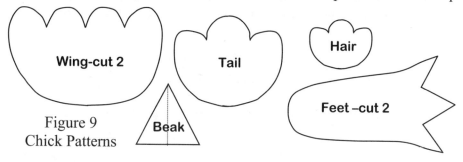

Wing-cut 2

Tail

Hair

Feet –cut 2

Figure 9
Chick Patterns

Beak

Slinky Critters

Grades 1-5

These funny looking critters are really fun to make.

Holiday Variations: Use holiday appropriate colors

Supply List

Craft Foam—bright color
Styrofoam Balls—1½ inch
Chenille Stems—2 colors
Wiggly Eyes—10mm
Acrylic Paint—bright color
Small Glass Bowl
Toothpicks

Ruler, Ink Pen, Scissors, Glue

Advance Preparations:

▶ Cut foam into 1-inch x 12-inch strips.
▶ Make a mark down the middle of each strip every 1¼-inch.
▶ To make holes for the Chenille to go through, crease the foam at each mark and cut a small slit where the mark is.
▶ For antennas, cut chenille into 3-inch lengths.
▶ Cut the other color of chenille in half (6-inch long) for the body.
▶ Paint Styrofoam balls for the head by pouring a small amount of paint in the bottom of a glass bowl. Roll the Styrofoam ball around in the paint with your finger until completely covered. Stick with a toothpick, remove from the paint, and stick the toothpick into an inverted Styrofoam plate. Let dry.

Time Saving Tip
To speed up the drying time, simply place the plate and balls in the microwave. Cook for 30 seconds and repeat until dry.

How To Make Them:

1. Make a little bend in one of the ends of the long piece of chenille.
2. Take the other end of the chenille and thread it through the slits in the craft foam. Make sure to bend the foam back and forth accordion style to make the body.

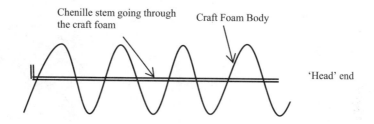

Chenille stem going through the craft foam

Craft Foam Body

'Head' end

3. Cut about 1-1½ inches off the 'head' end of the chenille. There should be about ¾-inch sticking out to attach the head to.
4. Slightly bend up the chenille stem and poke it into the Styrofoam ball 'head'.
5. Glue on the eyes.
6. Fold the small pieces of chenille in half to form a V and poke into the top of the 'head" to make antennas.

Variation:

- Try using felt for the critter body instead of craft foam.

Pastel Butterflies   Grades 1-5

These colorful butterflies are so fun and easy to make, you might have trouble making only one.

Supply List

Coffee Filters
Food Coloring
Small Dishes
Wiggly Eyes—5 mm
Black Permanent Marker
Snap Clothes Pins
Chenille Stems-any color

Paper Plates, Paper Towels

Advance Preparations:

▶ To prepare the 'paint' for this project, put 2-3 Tablespoons of water in a small dish and add 3-6 drops of food coloring. The more food coloring you add the darker the color will be. Repeat for each color. Depending on the number of children that are at the party, make additional 'paint' so there isn't a long wait.

▶ Cut chenille stems in half (6-inch long).

How To Make Them:
Dyeing Instructions

1. Fold the coffee filter so it forms a triangle. There is no right or wrong way to fold these. It is fun to experiment with the folds and dipping to see how it affects the colors.

2. Quickly dip a corner or side in one color. Turn to another corner or side and dip in a second color. Repeat with a third color. The color is absorbed very fast, so use a very quick dipping action.

3. Carefully unfold and place on a paper plate. Use a paper towel to remove excess water.

4. Let dry (about 20 minutes). To dry it quickly, put plate and dyed filter in the microwave and cook for 1 minute.

5. To make the butterfly wings, gather the filter in the middle so it looks like a bow tie.
6. Open the clothes pin and use it to grab all the gathers.
7. Arrange the filter so they look like 'wings'.
8. To make the antennas, bend the chenille in half to form a V and make small loops on both ends.
9. Open the clothes pin and let it grab the middle of the antennas.

Suggestions:

- Since these are so inexpensive to make, let the children make several and then pick the one or two that they want to use for their butterfly's wings.

Variations:

- Use water color or markers (not permanent markers) to color the coffee filters.
- Use a paint brush to apply the colors. This will let you add colorful dots to your butterfly's wings.
- Instead of using chenille for the antennas, simply use a heavy weight paper or construction paper and cut it into thin 6-inch pieces.

Did You Know?

...that butterflies taste with their feet? Their taste sensors are located in their feet and by standing on their food they can taste it.

Pastel Flowers   Grades 1-5

These easy flowers can be made into a colorful Spring or Easter bouquet for someone special.

Supply List

Coffee Filters
Food Coloring
Small Dishes
Snap Clothes Pins
Green Chenille Stems
Green Bump Chenille Stems

Paper Plates, Paper Towels

Advance Preparations:

► To prepare the 'paint' for this project, put 2-3 Tablespoons of water in a small dish and add 3-6 drops of food coloring. The more food coloring you add the darker the color will be. Repeat for each color. Depending on the number of children that are at the party, make additional 'paint' so there isn't a long wait.
► Cut chenille stems in half (6-inches long).
► Cut bump chenille stems in half (6-inches long).

How To Make Them:

1. To color the flowers, follow the "Dyeing Instructions" on page 34.
2. Gently fold a colored coffee filter in fourths and pinch and twist the pointed end. Only pinch about ¾ inch.
3. To attach the stem to the flower, wrap the chenille stem tightly around the twisted tip.
4. To help make the 'flower petals' open up, squeeze the flower with an upward motion several times. Adjust the 'petals' by creasing the edges until it looks like a flower.
5. Wrap the middle of the bump chenille piece around the stem for the leaves.
6. Group flowers together to make a bouquet.

Tubular Bracelets　Grades 1-5

Girls of all ages will have fun making these bracelets.

Supply List

Clear Plastic Tubing
　(see note below)
Paper
Glitter and/or **Small Beads**

Clear Tape, Scissors

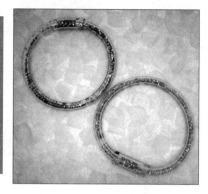

Notes:

Tubing: Clear plastic tubing is available in the plumbing section of most hardware stores. You will need two sizes, one for the bracelet itself and one as a fastener. We used 1/4" OD (outside diameter) for our bracelets and 3/8" OD for the fasteners. Just make sure the smaller tube fits securely in the larger tube. For each bracelet you will need 8" to 10" of the bracelet tubing and at least 1" of the fastener tubing. The tubing is surprisingly inexpensive, so buy plenty.

Glitter and Beads: Glitter works well in these bracelets. If you want to use small beads or gemstones, make sure they are small enough to fit inside your bracelet tubing.

How To Make Them:

1. Cut the bracelet tubing in 8 to10-inch lengths and the fastener tubing into 1-inch lengths.
2. Attach the two pieces of tubing together to form the bracelet.
3. Try on the bracelet and if it is too big, take it apart and cut it to size. Make sure it is big enough to slip over your hand.
4. Cut the paper into 3-inch squares and bend to make a funnel with a very small tip opening. Secure with tape.
5. Unfasten the tubing, and place a piece of tape over one end. Use the funnel to pour the glitter into the other end. Use your fingers to add the beads. Shake as you go to move them through the bracelet.
6. Remove the tape and **securely** refasten the tubings together.

Balloon Yo-Yos   Grades K-5

IDEA #20

The children will have a great time playing with these after they make them.

Holiday Variation: Buy holiday colored balloons .

Supply List

Balloons—round 9-inch
Permanent Markers—fun colors
Large Rubber Bands
Water
—————
Scissors

How To Make Them:

1. Attach the mouth of the balloon over the end of a faucet, and while holding it securely in place, turn on the water and fill it up with water. Stop when the balloon doubles in size.
2. Pinch the neck of the balloon tightly and remove from the faucet.
3. While still pitching the balloon, begin to blow it up and slowly release your hold. The first time you try this you will probably get wet, but don't give up. The balloon should be ¾ full of air.
4. Tie the end of the balloon with a knot.
5. With the markers, decorate the balloon.
6. Cut the rubber band and tie <u>securely</u> with a double knot to the end of the balloon.

WARNING: Always use caution when using balloons around small children. Make sure you discard any broken balloon pieces immediately.

> Balloon Yo-Yo's are very inexpensive, so buy lots of balloons and let the children make more than one.

Buggy Note Holders Grades K-5

These super easy note holders will be a useful addition to any refrigerator .

Supply List

Pompoms—1-inch assorted colors
Wiggly Eyes—7 mm
Chenille Stems—assorted colors
Clothespins—spring type
Magnetic Tape

Scissors, Glue

Advance Preparations:
▶ For the antennas, cut the chenille into 3-inch lengths.
▶ Cut the magnetic tape into 1-inch lengths.

How To Make Them:
1. Glue four pompoms onto the top of a clothespin. They should be tight against each other.
2. Glue the wiggly eyes to the first pompom. For placement, use the picture as a guide.
3. Fold the chenille antennas in half to form a V, add a dab of glue to the tip of the V, and push into the top of the first pompom.
4. Peel the backing off the magnet and stick to the bottom of clothes pin.

Did You Know?

Many insects can carry 50 times their own body weight. This would be like an adult person lifting two heavy cars full of people.

IDEA #22

Pencil Toppers   Grades K-6

Make a colorful pencil extra special by adding one of these fun toppers to it.

Supply List

Chenille Stems—bright colors
Craft Foam—bright colors
Pencils—colorful
Wiggly Eyes—7 mm

Scissors, Glue, Hot Glue Gun, Pen, Tracing Paper, Cardboard, Paper Hole Punch

Advance Preparations:

► Cut craft foam into 1½-inch square pieces. These will be the center pieces and each child will need one of these.

► Using the tracing paper, copy the shapes in Figure 10 and cut out. Copy these patterns onto the piece of cardboard and cut out.

► Using the cardboard pattern, trace the patterns onto the craft foam. Cut apart.

► With the hole punch, make mini circles by punching holes in leftover pieces of craft foam. If you are using wiggly eyes, you will not need these.

► Cut chenille stems in half.

► NOTE: <u>For young children</u>: cut out all the pieces for them. This way they just have to glue the pieces together.

How To Make Them:

1. Cut the 1½-inch square pieces of craft foam into circles.
2. Following the pattern on the craft foam, cut out the flowers.
3. Glue the circle piece to the middle of the flower.
4. If you have wiggly eyes, glue them onto the circle piece and draw a smile under them to make a happy face.
5. For a regular flower, glue 4-6 mini circles to the middle of the circle piece.

6. Using the picture as a guide, wrap the chenille stem around the top of the pencil. Make sure you leave 1-inch of chenille stem at the top to attach the flower to.
7. To finish them off, let an adult glue the flower to the top of the chenille stem with a hot glue gun.

Variations:

♦ Make the pencil toppers the shape of a Valentine for Valentines Day, Shamrocks for St. Patrick Day, Leaves or Pumpkins for Fall Parties...you get the idea....use your imagination and top the pencils with most any simple design.

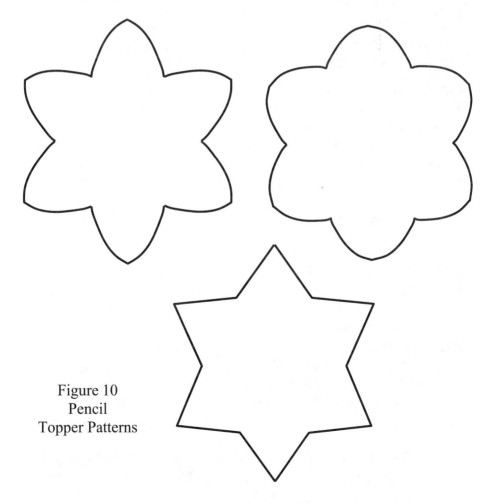

Figure 10
Pencil
Topper Patterns

Balloon Walkers

(IDEA #23)

Grades 3-5

These cute little guys will bring a smile to anyone that is special enough to receive one.

Supply List

Balloon
Construction Paper-2 colors
Paper
String
Black Permanent Marker
Velcro Dots

Scissors, Ruler, Glue

Advance Preparations:

► Cut construction paper into 1-inch strips making them as long as possible. Use a paper cutter if you have access to one.
► Cut the string into 18-inch lengths.
► Blow up the balloons and tie into a knot.

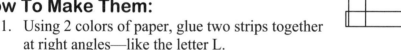

How To Make Them:

1. Using 2 colors of paper, glue two strips together at right angles—like the letter L.
2. Fold the bottom strip over the top strip (accordion style) and repeat until the strips end. Glue the last fold.
3. Repeat steps 1-2 with the other strips of paper until you have folded enough pieces for the arms and legs of your "Walker". If you use large balloons, you will need to tape or glue two accordion folded pieces together to make them long enough for the arms and legs.
4. Stick a Velcro dot on the end of each arm and leg piece, and carefully stick the other side of the dot to the balloon. Make sure the arms and legs are in the right position because once stuck to the balloon, the dots can not be moved.
5. Draw a funny face on the balloon with a black marker.
6. Finish it by tying a piece of string to the top of the balloon.

Flower Pens & Pot   Grades K-5

Let it be spring all year-round with this fun party favor. They make great gifts too!

Supply List
Artificial Flowers—large
Ink Pens
Floral Tape—green
Clay Pot—4-inch
Stickers
Pinto Beans—dry

Old Scissors, Tape

Advance Preparations:
▶ Trim each flower so there is only about 4-inchs of stem below the flower. It is ok to have a couple leaves on each stem.
▶ Place a piece of tape over the hole in the bottom of the clay pots.

How To Make Them:
1. Decorate the clay pot with stickers.
2. Fill the clay pot almost full with pinto beans.
3. Starting right below the flower, place the top of the pen next to the stem and wrap the florist tape around both the stem and the pen. Continue this spiral wrapping down to the end of the pen and cut the tape. If there are leaves on the stem, make sure you let them stick out of the tape and wrap around them. The pen should be completely covered with tape, except for the writing tip.
4. Stick the flower pens into the decorated pot.

Suggestions:
• Add any leftover buds or greenery to the pots (like we did).
• Use permanent markers to write names on the pots. They can also be used to decorate the pots.

IDEA #25 # **Funny Hairy's**   Grades K-5

Kids will have fun creating a funny-faced pot that will magically begin to grow hair in just a couple of days.

Supply List
Styrofoam Cups—large 8 oz.
Styrofoam Plates—small
Potting Soil
Grass or **Wheat Seeds**
Permanent Markers
Toothpicks
White Paper

Spoons, Scissors, Glue,
Pencil, Water

Advance Preparations:
▶ Poke two holes in the bottom of each cup with a pencil.
▶ Cut the white paper into 1½" x 2" pieces.

How To Make Them:
1. With the permanent markers, draw a face on the cup.
2. With a large spoon, fill the cup almost full with potting soil.
3. Sprinkle grass seeds all over the top of the soil.
4. Cover the grass seeds with a thin layer of soil (barely cover it).
5. Water and place on a small Styrofoam plate.
6. On a small piece of paper write "Water Me Every Day!"
7. Glue the toothpick to the back of the piece of paper.
8. Put the little sign in the soil and place in a sunny window.

Suggestions:
• About two weeks before the party, make a Funny Hairy so that it will have time to grow. This way the children will get to see what their project will eventually look like.
• Ask your local nursery for fast growing grass seed or wheat seed.
• Use printed face stickers instead of the permanent markers.

Dandy Candy Airplanes

Grades 1-5

Looking for a fun party favor just for boys? Try making these sweet little airplanes.

Supply List

Gum—sticks
Rolls of Candy—Smarties
Lifesavers™ — large
    individually wrapped
Rubber bands—thin, 3½-inch
Stickers—tiny (optional)
Glue

How To Make Them:

1. Glue two sticks of gum together to make the wings. Make sure the paper seams are not showing on the outside.
2. Unwrap two Lifesavers™ 'wheels' and thread a rubber band through them.
3. Lay the gum wings on top and put the end of the rubber band over the end of the gum. Repeat on the other side.
4. Move the rubber bands towards the center leaving a 1-inch space.
5. Push the roll of candy through the hole above the wheels and under the wings (see picture).
6. Move the wheels up beside the body.

Suggestion:

♦ A second set of hands can be a lot of help with this project. Consider having the children work as teams.

Variations:

• Use a small pack of gum (5 sticks) for the wings.
• Make a biplane by using two sets of wings (4 total sticks). The roll of candy will need to go between the two wings and the wheels will be together.

Silly "Its"

Grades K-5

Let the children use their imagination when creating these funny looking critters.

Supply List
Craft Foam—bright colors
Styrofoam Balls—1½ inch
Chenille Stems—right colors
Wiggly Eyes—10mm
Wire—black
Acrylic Paint—bright colors
Small Glass Bowl
Toothpicks

Scissors, Glue, Large Sucker

Advance Preparations:
▶ For antennas, cut chenille into 3-inch lengths and the wire into 6-inch lengths. Each "IT" will need 2 lengths.

▶ Cut craft foam into 2-inch squares. These will be the feet.

▶ Paint Styrofoam balls for the head by pouring a small amount of paint in the bottom of a glass bowl. Roll the Styrofoam ball around in the paint with your finger until completely covered. Stick with a toothpick, remove from the paint, and stick the toothpick into an inverted Styrofoam plate. Let dry. **TIP:** To speed up the drying time, simply place the plate and balls in the microwave. Cook for 30 seconds and repeat until dry.

How To Make Them:
1. Cut a square of craft foam into 2 feet shapes. Glue to the ball.
2. Wrap the black wire tightly around a sucker stick to look like a coil. Remove and poke into the top of the ball for antennas.
3. Glue the wiggly eyes onto "IT's" head. Done!

Variation:
♦ Use 1½ inch Pompoms for "IT's" head. Double the length of the antennas and fold in half to make a V instead of cutting apart. Glue to the top of "IT's" head.

Patriotic Windsock   Grades K-3

IDEA #28

Show your pride by hanging this windsock outside where everyone can see it. But take it inside if it's going to rain.

Supply List

Poster Board—white
Stickers and Markers
Yarn—red <u>or</u> white <u>or</u> blue
Crepe Paper Streamers—
  red, blue

Scissors, Stapler, Glue Stick, Hole Punch, Ruler, Tape

Advance Preparations:

▶ Cut the poster board into 11"x14" pieces. You should be able to make two windsocks out of one piece of poster board.

▶ On the long side of each piece of poster board, punch three holes approximately 3½-inches apart.

▶ Cut the streamers into 24" lengths. Need 4 for each windsock.

▶ Cut the yarn into 12" lengths. Need 3 pieces for each windsock.

How To Make Them:

1. Turn the poster board so the holes are at the top.
2. Decorate the poster board with markers and stickers.
3. Turn the poster board over and tape 4 streamers along the bottom edge of the poster board. Try to space them evenly.
4. Turn back over and with the glue stick, place glue along the long edge, bend into a tube shape, overlap the two ends and hold in place until dry. Staple the ends if necessary.
5. Take three pieces of yarn and tie one end of each piece through each hole.
6. Gather the remaining ends and tie together.

Variations:

• Use bright spring colors and decorate with flowers, or modify the colors and decorations for any holiday.

(IDEA #29) **Smiley Play Dough**   Grades K-3

Let the children use cookie cutters to play with their dough and then they can turn it into a cute take-home gift.

Holiday Variation: Use orange dough and draw a jack-o-lantern face on the plastic wrap. Top off with a green piece of curling ribbon.

Supply List
Play Dough—see recipe
Clear Plastic Wrap
Yellow Curling Ribbon
Black Permanent Markers
Food Coloring—yellow

Saucepan, Large Spoon, Scissors, Zip Top Plastic Bag

Advance Preparations:
▶ Cut the yellow curling ribbon into 12-inch pieces.
▶ Cut the plastic wrap into 9" x 9" pieces.
▶ To make 1 cup of play dough (enough for two children):
  1 cup **Corn Starch**
  2 cups **Baking Soda**
  1¼ cup **Cold Water**
In a sauce pan, combine water, baking soda, corn starch and a few drops of yellow food coloring. Cook over low heat, stirring constantly, until a ball of dough forms. Cool the dough for 5 minutes, and then knead it with your hands until it is smooth. Place in a plastic bag until the party.

How To Make Them:
1. Roll a piece of play dough into a round ball.
2. Place the ball into the center of a piece of plastic wrap. Pull the corners of the plastic wrap over the top of the play dough.
3. Tie the yellow ribbon around the gathered plastic wrap just above the play dough ball. Curl the ribbon with the scissors.
4. With the black marker, draw a Happy Face on the plastic wrap.

Fall Painted Pots Grades K-5

Paint these colorful pots early in the party, sit them in the sunshine, and they'll be dry before the party's over.

Holiday Variation: Paint the pot red with white snowflakes, or valentines, or use bright colors and flowers for a spring party.

Supply List

Clay Pots—4-inch
Acrylic Paint—yellow, white
Paint Brushes
Black Permanent Marker
Cellophane—clear
Raffia or Ribbon—orange
Candy Corn

3 Small Bowls, Scissors,
Newspapers

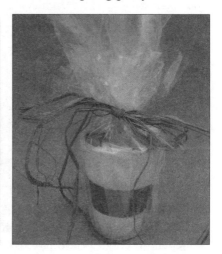

Advance Preparations:
▶ Cover the painting area with newspaper.
▶ Pour the yellow and white paint in two small bowls.
▶ Pour water in the third small bowl.

How To Make Them:
1. Write your name on the bottom of the pot with a black marker.
2. Paint the top third of the clay pot yellow.
3. Paint the lower third of the clay pot white.
4. Put it in the sunshine or in front of a fan to help it dry faster.
5. When dry, fill with candy corn.
6. Place the pot in the middle of a sheet of cellophane, gather it up evenly around the pot, and twist.
7. With a partner, wrap the raffia or ribbon around the twisted cellophane and tie into a bow. For younger children, let the child hold the pot while an adult ties the bow.
8. Trim the cellophane, if necessary, so there is only about 4 to 5-inches above the pot.

Leaf People   Grades K-5

Celebrate the fall season with these super easy to make bendable characters. They can hang around all fall.

Supply List

Craft Foam—red, yellow, orange
Chenille Stems—any color
Black Permanent Marker

Paper Hole Punch, Pen, Scissors, Tracing Paper, Cardboard

Advance Preparations:

▶ Using the tracing paper, copy the Leaf pattern in Figure 11 and cut out. Copy these patterns onto the piece of cardboard and cut out.
▶ Using the cardboard pattern, trace the Leaf pattern onto the different colors of craft foam. Cut the leaves apart.
▶ Using a paper hole punch, make holes in each leaf for the arms and legs. The * in Figure 11 shows where these holes should go.
▶ Cut chenille in half (6-inches). If you make leaf bodies that are larger than 3"x 3", use a whole chenille stem for the arms and legs.
▶ Cut the left-over pieces of craft foam into small pieces (1"x 1") that can be cut into hands and feet. Each child will need 4 pieces.

NOTE: <u>For young children</u>, or <u>to save time</u>, cut out the body pieces. This way the children just have to put the pieces together. <u>Older children</u> can make their own leaf patterns and punch their own holes.

How To Make Them:

1. Cut the leaf bodies out of the craft foam.
2. Cut the small pieces of craft foam into 2 hands and 2 feet shapes.
3. With the paper punch, make holes in the end of each hand and foot.

4. For the arms, thread a chenille stem in one arm hole and out the other.
5. Pull both ends to make the arms the same length (see picture).
6. Repeat step 4 for the legs. After threading the chenille through the holes, pull them down so they are in the position of legs.
7. Add the hands and feet by threading the ends through the holes and then bend the very ends to keep the pieces in place.
8. Draw a funny face on the leaf with the marker. Wiggly eyes can also be used.

Suggestion:

- Draw your own leaf patterns or let the children draw and cut out their own.

Variations:

♦ Make the bodies the shape of a Valentine for Valentines Day, or Flowers for Spring and Summer parties.

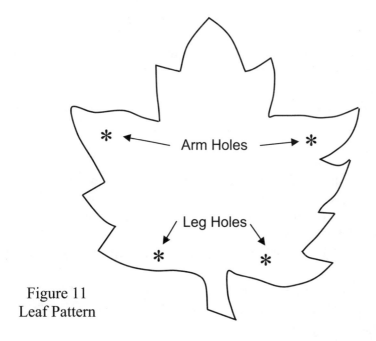

Figure 11
Leaf Pattern

IDEA #32 # Scarecrow Treat Bag Grades K-3

Young children enjoy making these cute fall treat bags.

Supply List

Paper Plates—9-inch
Paint—yellow
Yarn—dark orange
Felt—red
Plaid Material—fall colors
Paper Sacks—brown
Black Permanent Markers

Scissors, Paper Punch, Glue,
Tape, Paint Brush, Pencil

Advance Preparations:

▶ Fold a paper plate in half and using the picture as a guide, draw two ovals for the eyes on the bottom half of the backside of a paper plate.

▶ Paint everything yellow but the eyes.

▶ When the paint has dried, draw the mouth and eyes on each plate with a black marker. Use the picture as an example.

▶ Cut the plate into two pieces along the fold line.

▶ Place the two halves back together, lining up the edges, and tape together. Make sure both of the yellow sides are showing.

▶ Punch holes about every inch around the outside of the paper plate.

▶ Cut yarn into 40-inch lengths.

▶ Tightly wrap a small piece of tape around the end of the yarn. This will work like a needle.

▶ Thread the yarn through the corner hole and pull until you have a 9-inch 'tail' left. Tie a knot.

▶ Cut the brown paper bag (the parts without printing) into 1¼-inch by 6-inch strips.

▶ Cut felt into 1½-inch triangles.

▶ Cut the plaid material into 2½-inch by 8-inch strips. Tie a knot in the middle so it looks like a bow tie.

How To Make Them:

1. With the needle end of the yarn, lace through the holes by putting the yarn down through the top hole, out the backside, and then back through the top of the next hole. Continue until the plates are 'sewn' together.
2. Remove the tape and tie the two ends of the yarn together.
3. Glue the red felt triangle on for the nose.
4. Make the hair by cutting the strip of brown paper into short narrow strips (¼-inch x 1¼-inch). Glue these strips along the top edge of the paper plate. They look best if they are glued unevenly and if part of them hang over the top edge.
5. Glue the bow to the bottom center of the plate.
6. Fill with candy and enjoy!

Did You Know?

Scarecrows are made to keep birds out of the family garden.

Kitty Treats   Grades K-3

This easy craft can double as a place card, which can be used to save a seat at the party table.

Holiday Variation: Draw a collar around the cat's neck and place a holiday sticker (i.e. heart, shamrock, bow, flower) in the middle of the collar for a tag.

Supply List

Craft Foam—white and black
White Gel Pen
Black Fine Tip Marker
Candy—miniature boxes
Glue
Scissors

Tracing Paper, Cardboard

Advance Preparations:

▶ Using the tracing paper, copy the patterns in Figure 12 and cut out. Copy these patterns onto the piece of cardboard and cut out.
▶ Using the cardboard patterns, trace the patterns onto the craft foam, and cut a part.
▶ NOTE: For young children: cut out the body pieces for them. This way they just have to glue the pieces together.

How To Make Them:

1. Cut the two body parts out of the craft foam.
2. Using the pen or marker, draw a face on the cat. If you plan to use them as table place cards, have the children write their name below the cat's head. You can also draw a collar and add a sticker tag if you want to.
3. Glue the front and back pieces of the cat to the box of candy.
4. Hold the pieces in place for a minute or two. The cat should now be able to stand alone.

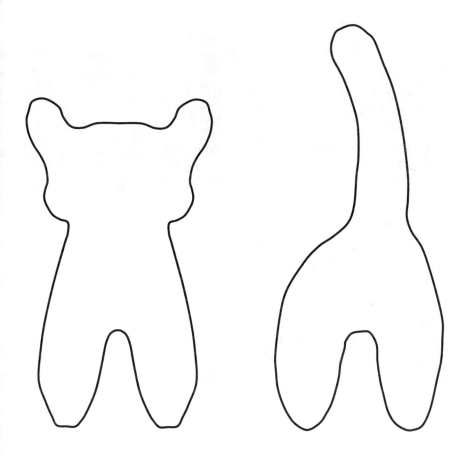

Figure 12
Cat Body Patterns

Slime

#34

Grades 2-5

This slimy dough will be a big hit at any party...and the most fun is having the children make it themselves.

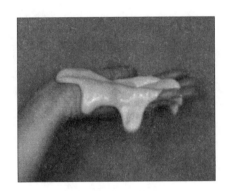

Supply List

White Glue
Baby Powder
Borax Powder
Water
Green Food Coloring
Plastic Spoons
Plastic Soup Bowls
Funnel
Measuring Cups
Measuring Spoons
2—1 liter **Plastic Bottles**
Zip-Top Plastic Bags

Advance Preparations:

▶ With the funnel, pour the following ingredients into each plastic bottle:

Potion #1: ½ cup baby powder
2½ cups white glue
2 cups water
Green food coloring (add until it's **light** green)

Potion #2: 2 tablespoons borax powder
2 cups **warm** water

▶ Label the bottles Potion #1 and Potion #2.

On the day of the party:

▶ Set up an area where the children will make the slime. If possible, set up near a sink.

▶ Cover the 'slime area' with newspaper for easy clean up. Since the children will get their hands dirty, (that is the fun part) have baby wipes available to clean their hands if a sink is not available.

How To Make It:

1. At the 'slime area', give each child a soup bowl and spoon.
2. Pour 1/4 cup of Potion #1 into each bowl.
3. With their spoons, they will add 2 to 3 teaspoons of Potion #2 to Potion #1. Stir after each spoonful. By the time the third spoonful has been added, the liquid should change into a dough like substance.
4. Instruct the children to pick up the mixture and knead it with their hands until the liquid is absorbed and is no longer sticky. They can now play with it just like play dough.
5. Place the Slime in a zip-top plastic bag and have them wash up. Instruct the children to place the Slime in their bags after each use. It will last longer.

Helpful Hints:

• Mixing the two potions together is not an exact science. The secret is to add Potion #2 **slowly** to Potion #1, making sure to stir them together as you are pouring. If the mixture becomes hard, not slimy, you have added too much of Potion #2. Throw it away and start over.

• When coloring your Slime, use only a **few** drops of food coloring. Too much food coloring will discolor the children's hands.

• Tell the children to refrigerate their Slime to help keep it fresh. Slime usually lasts between 7 to 10 days, depending upon use.

• Plastic water bottles work well for the potions.

• Make sure Potion #2 is **warm**.

IDEA #35 # Sugar Art   **Grades K-5**

This colorful project will be a real hit at any party!

Supply List

Baby Food Jars <u>with</u> **Lids**
Powder Food Coloring—at
 least 2 colors
Black Permanent Marker
Sugar
_____
Large Zip-Top Plastic Bags,
2 Large Bowls, Craft Sticks,
Plastic Spoons

Advance Preparations:

▶ Remove all labels and glue from the baby food jars.
▶ Fill all of the jars with sugar.
▶ Take a few of the jars and pour into a zip-top bag. Add one color of powder food coloring to the bag, seal, and shake until well mixed. Add additional food coloring until it is the color you want.
▶ Repeat this process with the second color of food coloring.
▶ Continue to color the remaining sugar.
▶ With the permanent marker, color the lids black.

How To Make Them:

1. Pour the bags of sugar into two large bowls.
2. With a spoon, layer the sugar, one color on top of the other. As the layers are made, push a craft stick down the inside walls of the jar to create designs.
3. Continue layering the sugar until the jar is **completely** full. This will keep the layers from getting mixed together. Place the lid on the jar and secure tightly.

Suggestion:

• Powdered food coloring is usually available at cake supply stores and on-line. If you can not find it, use dry tempera paint instead and use salt instead of sugar...this way the children won't eat it.

Pine Cone Bird Feeder Grades K-5

This easy project is a real treat for our fine feathered friends during the cold winter months. Be sure to hang it outside on a tree where you can see it from a window.

Supply List

Large Pine Cones
Plastic Knives
String
Small Bowls
Peanut Butter
Birdseed

Scissors, Newspapers, Plastic Sandwich Bags, Wet Washcloth or Baby Wipes

Advance Preparations:

▶ With the scissors, cut the string into 10-inch pieces.
▶ Tie the string tightly around the top of each pine cone.
▶ Cover the area with newspapers for fast and easy clean up.
▶ Pour the peanut butter and birdseed into small bowls.

How To Make Them:

1. Take a pine cone and, with a plastic knife, spread peanut butter between the petals of the pinecone.
2. Next, roll the pine cone in the birdseed. With your hands, gently press more birdseed all around the pine cone until the peanut butter is completely covered.
3. When done, place the pine cone in a plastic sandwich bag.
4. Use the wet washcloth or baby wipes to clean your hands.
5. Tell the children to hang their pine cone bird feeder in a tree where it can be seen from a window. That way they can watch the birds enjoy their winter treat.

Cookies In A Jar

IDEA #37

Grades 1-5

Make a batch of these cookies for your party and then let the children make these to take home with them.

Supply List
Wide Mouth Canning Jar-quart
Fabric—fun small print
Raffia—natural
Paper—fun light colored
Cookie Ingredients—see recipe

Spoons, Bowls (6), Pen, 1 Hole Paper Punch, Scissors, Measuring Spoons, Measuring Cups

Advance Preparations:
▶ Wash and dry the jars.
▶ Copy the recipe in Figure 13 onto the paper. Make one for each jar. You can also use preprinted recipe cards instead of the paper.
▶ Punch a hole in the corner of each recipe card.
▶ Cut the Raffia into 2 feet lengths. Cut at least two for each jar.
▶ Cut the material into 8-inch round pieces. We used a mixing bowl (turned upside down) to trace around and then cut it out.

On The Day Of The Party:
▶ Place the following ingredients in separate bowls. You will need the amount in the ( ) for each jar. For example, if you are filling **5** jars, then pour at least 10 cups of flour into a bowl.

Flour	(2 cups)
Baking Soda	(½ teaspoon)
Salt	(¼ teaspoon)
Packed Brown Sugar	(¾ cup)
Sugar	(¼ cup)
M & M's	(2 cups)

How To Make Them:

1. Layer all of the dry ingredients in the canning jar in the order listed. It is important that you pack down, with a spoon, all of the ingredients, especially the brown sugar. Make sure you use enough M & M's to fill the jar all the way to the top.
2. Screw the lid on the jar.
3. Center the round piece of fabric over the lid.
4. To secure the fabric, take two pieces of raffia (together), wrap tightly around the lip of the jar and tie into a knot. The fabric should be under the raffia.
5. Thread the raffia through the hole in the recipe card and tie the ends into a nice big bow. **Note:** Small children will probably need help with these last two steps.

Suggestions:

- It really doesn't matter in what order you layer the ingredients. The important thing is that you place the right quantity of each ingredient in each jar.
- Use your own favorite cookie recipe. Just put all the dry ingredients in the jar and write the rest of your recipe on the recipe card.
- Use fancy cut scissors to cut around the recipe card. You can also use them to cut-out the lid covers, if they will cut fabric.

M & M Cookies

To these ingredients add:
        3/4 cup margarine, softened
        1 egg
        1 teaspoon vanilla

Pour contents of the jar into a large bowl and mix well. Add the margarine and mix until well blended. Beat together the egg and vanilla and add to the batter. Shape the dough into 1-inch balls and place 2-inches apart on a cookie sheet. In a 350° oven, bake for 10 to 14 minutes, or until the edges are lightly browned.

Figure 13   Cookie Recipe

(IDEA #38) **Shrinking Art**   Grades K-5

Trace a fun picture, color it and then watch it shrink.
Make them into ornaments, necklaces or pins.

Holiday Variation: Simply find a picture or card with a large design that represent your are celebrating and trace it.

Supply List
'Shrink It' Plastic—opaque
Colored Pencils
Picture or Card—large design
Sandpaper—fine
Paper—white
Ribbon, Magnet, Pin or Mini
    Clothespin
_____
Scissors, Tape, Hole Punch,
Foil, Cookie Sheet, Oven

Advance Preparations:
▶ With the sandpaper, sand each sheet of 'Shrink It' plastic up and down and across corner to corner. This will help the colors adhere to the plastic better.
▶ Find a picture or card that is drawn with a simple design (or use the ones in Figures 14 and 15) They shrink 2/3, so 3"x 5" or larger designs work best. Look in coloring books or at greeting cards for designs.
▶ Cut the 'Shrink It' plastic so it just covers the design.

How To Make Them:
1. Place the 'Shrink It' plastic, with the sanded side up, on top of the picture and outline with a pencil.
2. Put a white piece of paper under the 'Shrink It' plastic and color with colored pencils.
3. Cut out the design. Punch a hole in the top of it if you are going to use it as a necklace or a hanging ornament.

4. Place on a foil lined cookie sheet and bake in a 250° to 275° oven for about 5 minutes or until it lays flat. You can't overcook it.
5. Let it cool and then tie on the ribbon, or attach the pin, magnet or mini clothespin to the back of the shrink art.

Figure 14
Shrinking Art Snowman
Sample Pattern

Figure 15
Shrinking Art
Butterfly Sample Pattern

Reindeer Ornaments Grades K-3

This ornament looks great hanging on the Christmas tree.

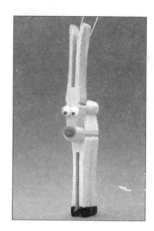

Supply List

Clothespins—flat type
String
Wiggly Eyes—7mm
Pompoms—red ¼-inch
Sandwich Bags

Black Marker, Scissors, Glue

Advance Preparations:

▶ Cut the string into 8-inch pieces.
▶ For each child, put a piece of string, 3 clothespins, two eyes and one pompom into a sandwich bag. This will help speed up the passing out of supplies on the day of the party.

How To Make Them:

1. Give each child a sandwich bag and some glue.
2. Start by gluing two of the clothespins together. Hold together for a minute or two. This will be the body.
3. Next, take the piece of string and knot the ends together. Glue one end of the string to the top end of the body.
4. The last clothespin will be the head and antlers. It will be glued to the body where the string has been placed. The string will be sandwiched between the head and the body. Glue the last clothespin to the body in an upside down position.
5. While the glue is drying, pass out a few permanent black markers. Have the children take turns coloring the hooves on their reindeer.
6. To complete their reindeer, glue on the eyes and nose.

Reindeer Treat Cups   Grades K-3

Fill these super easy treat cups with holiday candy for a fun take-home party gift.

> ## Supply List
> **Nut Cups**—large
> **Chenille Stems**—brown
> **Pompoms**—red—½-inch
> **Wiggly Eyes**—7mm
> **Spray Paint**—brown
> **Holiday Candy**
>
> **Scissors, Glue, 1 Hole Paper Punch, Newspapers**

Advance Preparations:
► In a well ventialted area, spread out the newspapers.
► Place a nut cup in the middle of the newspapers and turn upside down.
► Spray the bottom and sides of the cup with brown spray paint.
► Repeat with the remaining nut cups.
► When dry, punch 2 holes in each cup. The holes should be about 1½-inches apart and right below the top rim of the cup. See the picture above to help with placement.
► Cut the chenille stems in half with an old pair of scissors.

How To Make Them:
1. For the antlers, bend two chenille stems into zigzag shapes.
2. Fasten the antlers to the nut cup by poking the bottom of the antler through one of the holes, bend it up and then twist back around the antler.
3. Glue the two eyes below and in-between the two antlers.
4. Glue the pompom nose below the eyes.
5. Fill with candy.

IDEA #41 Bead Candy Canes   Grades K-3

These colorful candy canes will liven up any Christmas tree. They are so easy and inexpensive to make that each child will want to make more than one.

Supply List

Chenille Stems—white
Red Tri-Beads— 11mm
   (20 for each candy cane)
White Tri-Beads— 11mm
   (20 for each candy cane)

Scissors, Pliers

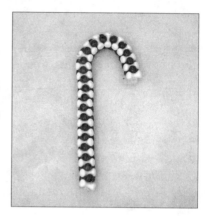

Advance Preparations:

▶ Place 20 red and 20 white beads in a sandwich bag. Each child will get a bag.

▶ Cut white pipe cleaners in half with the scissors.

▶ With the pliers, bend up one end of each chenille stem. This will keep the beads from sliding off. Place one piece in each bag.

How To Make Them:

1. Hand out a sandwich bag to each child.
2. Take the beads and chenille stem out of the bag.
3. Find the end of the chenille that is bent. This will be the bottom of the candy cane.
4. Make the candy cane by stringing the beads onto the chenille stem one at a time. Alternate between the red and the white beads.
5. When the chenille stem is full, bend the end of the pipe cleaner with the pliers so the beads will not fall off.
6. Bend the pipe cleaner into the shape of a candy cane and you're done.

(IDEA #42) **Puzzle Piece Wreath**   Grades K-5

These great looking refrigerator ornaments are the perfect gift for mom and dad, or a special friend.

Holiday Variation: For Valentines Day, use a heart shaped frame and cover with red or red and white puzzle pieces. Glue shinny heart sequins to the puzzle pieces for a special touch. For birthday parties, any shape of frame will work. Let your child pick the color(s) for the puzzle pieces and add shinny sequins to make it special.

Supply List

Puzzle—old 1,000 piece
Yarn—green
Bow Tie Macaroni
Craft Foam—red
Spray Paint—red and green gloss
Poster Board—green
Magnet Tape

Compass, Hot Glue Gun, Paper Punch, Pencils, Scissors, Glue, Waxed Paper

Advance Preparations:

▶ Spread out the puzzle pieces on waxed paper. Each child will need approximately 20 pieces. Spray with the green paint, making sure you get the sides of each piece. Let dry and spray again if necessary.

▶ Repeat the above step with the bow shaped macaroni, using the red spray paint.

▶ Cut the green yarn into 10-inch pieces.

▶ With the compass, draw 4-inch circles on the green poster board. Then draw 2½-inch circles inside the 4-inch circles. Cut apart. Using a sharp pair of scissors, poke a hole in the middle of the circle. This will help the children when cutting out the middle of the circle. For young children, or if you are short on time, cut the wreaths out.

▶ With the paper punch, cut "berries" out of the red craft foam. You will need 8-10 for each wreath.

On the day of the party:

▶ Set up a "glue station" where the children will have their bows and yarn glued onto their wreath by an adult using a hot glue gun.

How To Make Them:

1. Follow the drawn lines and cut out the circles to make the wreaths.
2. Glue about 20 puzzle pieces onto the green circle, first on one layer and then in a second layer, so the green poster board does not show.
3. Next, take the wreath to the "glue station" and have an adult hot glue the bow and yarn onto the wreath.
4. Glue on the red craft foam "berries" and you are done.
5. Peel the back off the magnet tape and attach to the back of your ornament.

Suggestion:

• If you have access to a digital camera and printer, take a picture of each child at the beginning of the party and print the pictures before they go home. Have them tape their picture to their new picture frame for a special take-home gift.

Time Saving Hint:

Check area arts and crafts stores for pre-cut wreath shapes. They usually are made of white poster board. Simply spray paint them along with the puzzle pieces.

IDEA #43) **Pasta Tree Ornaments** Grades 2+

Children will enjoy making these delightful tree ornaments. We have given you a number of different patterns, pick out one or two that you think the children will enjoy making.

Supply List
Wagon Wheel Pasta
Acrylic Paint
White String
Waxed Paper
Small Bowls
Paint Brush
White Glue
Toothpicks

Paper Towels, Glitter, Craft Foam, Colored Paper, Sequins

Advance Preparations:

▶ Decide which ornaments the children will be making. Depending on the ornament, each child will need the following materials:
Snowflake - 13 white pasta pieces and glitter.
Christmas Tree - 10 green and 1 brown pasta pieces, assorted colors of sequins, colored paper or craft foam.

▶ Paint the pasta pieces by following these simple directions:
1. In small bowls, mix 2 parts acrylic paint to 1 part water for each color. Make sure this mixture is at least ½-inch deep.
2. Place a piece of waxed paper on the table and put a paper towel that has been folded in half on top of it. This is where the pasta will dry after it is painted. Do this for each color.
3. Put pasta in the paint and with a paint brush cover all sides.
4. Take out of the paint with a toothpick and place on the paper towels to drain.
5. When the top is dry (looks dull) transfer to waxed paper to finish drying.

Advance Preparations (continued):

▶ Place all of the ornament pieces in a plastic bag for each child.

▶ On a large piece of paper, copy the ornament pattern (see Figure 16) so the children will have a pattern to look at. Make additional copies if necessary.

▶ Make a sample of the ornaments the children will be making.

How To Make Them:

1. Pass out one plastic bag with ornament supplies in it, and a piece of waxed paper to each child.
2. Give each child a small amount of glue on a small piece of waxed paper.
3. Have each child arrange their pasta as shown on the ornament pattern. The following directions will also help:

> **Snowflake:** Arrange 6 white pieces of pasta in a circle; place one in the center. Place 6 more pieces around the outer edge of the circle at each indentation.

> **Christmas Tree:** Arrange 9 green pasta pieces in a triangle with 4 pieces on each side and one in the middle. Place the brown piece of pasta at the bottom center of the triangle. Decorate as desired after it has dried.

4. Glue the pasta pieces together by dipping the pieces of pasta in the glue and sticking them together.
5. Allow to dry at least ½ hour.
6. Remove from the waxed paper and thread string through one of the wheels. Tie the ends together to form a hanger.
7. Decorate as desired with glitter, colored paper, craft foam or ribbon.

Did You Know?

There is a pasta museum in Potedassio, Italy filled with antique pasta-making tool and dried samples of pasta dating back 100 years.

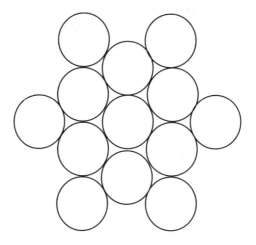

Snowflake

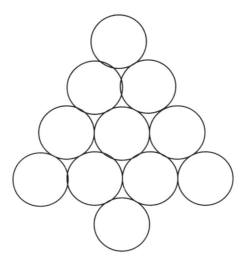

Christmas Tree

Figure 16
Pasta Ornament Patterns

(IDEA #44) **Candy Cane Reindeer** Grades K-3

This easy craft project turns a regular candy cane into a simple gift that any child would like to give.

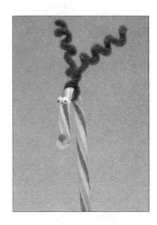

Supply List
Candy Canes—large
Chenille Stems—brown
Red Pompom—¼-inch
Wiggly Eyes—7mm

Glue, Pencil

How To Make Them:

1. The first step is to glue on the eyes. Hold them in place for a minute or two. Refer to the picture above for placement.
2. Next glue the red pompom nose to the end of the candy cane. Hold in place for a minute or two.
3. To make the antlers, bend the pipe cleaner in half and twist once around the top of the candy cane. With a pencil bend one side of the pipe cleaner around the pencil so it looks like a spring. Remove the pencil and stretch out the pipe cleaner. Repeat for the other half of the pipe cleaner.

Did You Know?

Reindeer and caribou are the only deer where males, females, and calves produce antlers. They grown new antlers every year.

(IDEA #45) Fuzzy Mice

Grades 2-5

These cute little mice make fun book markers, or clip onto your Christmas tree as a special little ornament.

Supply List
Pompoms—1½ inch
White Felt
Pink Felt
Red Felt
Black Thread
Wiggly Eyes—6mm
Metal Hair Clips

Scissors, Glue, Pen, Cardboard, Tracing Paper

Advance Preparations:
▶ With the tracing paper, copy the patterns in Figure 17 and cut out. Transfer the patterns to a piece of cardboard by tracing around the cut out patterns. Cut each pattern out.
▶ Trace the feet, head and tail patterns on the white felt and cut out.
▶ Trace the ear pattern onto the pink felt. You will need two for each mouse. Cut them out.
▶ Trace the nose pattern onto the red felt and cut out.
▶ Cut the black thread into one-inch pieces. Cut 3 for each mouse.

How To Make Them:
1. Using the picture as a guide for placement, glue three threads to the head piece and then glue the nose over the black threads.
2. Glue on the two pink ear pieces and the eyes.
3. Glue the feet to the bottom of the pompom.
4. Glue the tail under the back of feet.
5. Glue the head onto the middle front of the pompom. The feet should be showing right under the head.
6. Glue the hair clip to the bottom of the feet with the clip opening towards the front for the mouse.

Variation: For Christmas, glue a red ¼" ribbon bow, green felt holly leaves and a ⅛" bell to the middle of the tail.

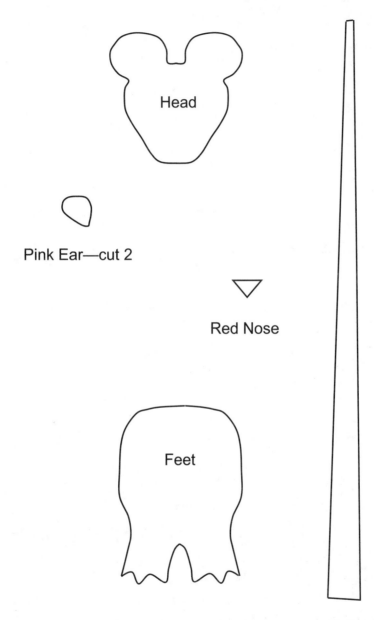

Head

Pink Ear—cut 2

Red Nose

Feet

Tail

Figure 17
Fuzzy Mice
Patterns

FUN PARTY GAMES

No party is complete without playing a couple of games. We have included a wide variety of games, but all of them will allow everyone to participate and no one will have to sit out. Some of them can become very rowdy, so to help keep the games under control, we have prepared the following suggestions.

Helpful Suggestions:
- To avoid accidents, make sure the game area is clear of all furniture, and breakable and sharp objects.
- Make sure the games are age appropriate by having your child try the skills that are required for each game.
- Divide the children into teams that are as even as possible. If there is an odd number of children, have one child go twice.
- With masking tape or a piece of string, make a starting line where the teams have to stay behind at all times.
- When a child has taken their turn, tell them to go to the back of the line, sit down and wait for the rest of their team to complete the relay. No team can win until everyone is sitting down!
- Plan on playing each game a couple of times, because the children will get better each time they play.
- Keep score and award everyone a prize when they are finished.
- Take it outside!

Have a great time!

Drawing Relay   Grades 1-5

This is a very simple game that results in some hilarious looking drawings!

Object Of The Game: To be the first team to draw all the parts on their character.

Variations: For Halloween draw a Witch, for Fall draw a Scarecrow, and for Christmas draw Santa Clause or a Snowman.

Supply List

Paper—Large sheets	Index Cards
Crayons	Masking Tape

Advance Preparations:

▶ For each team, draw the outline of the character on a piece of paper.

▶ Write on the index cards "parts" that can be drawn on the character (eyes, nose, ears, hat, buttons, shoes, bow, belt, etc.) Make sure each team has the same "parts" and there are enough for each child on each team.

On the day of the party:

▶ Tape the sheets of paper to a chalkboard or wall at one end of the room.

▶ Place the index cards and crayons under each sheet of paper.

How To Play:

1. Divide the children into two teams. Have the children form straight lines across the room from the papers.
2. Explain the object of the game.
3. On the signal "GO", the first child in each line will WALK to the picture, pick an index card and draw that item. The child then returns to their team, gives the crayon to the next child in line, and sits down at the end of the line.
4. The next child in line then picks an index card and draws that "part".
5. Play continues until everyone has had a turn drawing.
6. The team that completes their drawing first wins!

Suck It Up Relay   Grades 1-5

Be careful not to make your teammates laugh...it could cost you the game.

Object Of The Game: To be the first team to get all of their cotton balls in the container without using their hands.

Holiday Variations: Use holiday colored straws and containers.

Supply List

Cotton Ball—1 for each child
Drinking Straw—1 for each child
   (Cut straws in half for small children)
Colorful Buckets or **Containers**—2
Chairs—2

Advance Preparations:
On the day of the party:
▶ Place the two chairs at the far end of the room.
▶ Place the two empty containers on the chairs.

How To Play:
1. Divide the children into 2 teams and line them up in straight lines.
2. Give each child a straw and a cotton ball.
3. Explain the object of the game and demonstrate how to hold their cotton ball on their straw without using their hands (inhale through the straw). If a cotton ball drops on the floor they can only use their straw, NOT their hands, to pick it up.
4. The first person in each line places the straw in their mouth and breathes in so the cotton ball sticks to the end of their straw. While continuing to breath in, they will quickly WALK to the chair on the other side of the room and drop their cotton ball into the container. They will then turn around, WALK back to their line and tag the next person in line.
5. Play continues until everyone has dropped their cotton ball into the containers.

Balloon Pop Relay Grades K-5

This noisy relay game is always a big hit.

Object Of The Game: To be the first team to pop all of their balloons.

Holiday Variations: Use holiday colored balloons.

Supply List

Balloons—1 for each child
Trash Bags—2 large
Chairs—2

Advance Preparations:

▶ Blow up the balloons. Store in the large trash bags.
   On the day of the party:
   ▶ Place the two chairs at the far end of the room.

How To Play:

1. Divide the children into two teams. Position two "helpers" at the starting line and have the children form two lines behind them. Each of the "helpers" will have a bag of balloons.
2. Explain the object of the game and demonstrate how they will pop their balloon.
3. On the signal "GO", the first person in each line will take a balloon, run to the chair at the opposite end of the room, and sit on the balloon until it pops. The child then runs to tag the next person in line and sits down at the end of the line.
4. After being tagged, the next person in line takes a turn at popping a balloon.
5. Play continues until everyone has popped a balloon.

Variation:

• To make this more difficult for older children, give them a deflated balloon at the starting line. They must blow it up and tie it before running to the chair to pop it.
• Instead of running to the chairs, have the children place the balloon between their knees and hop.

IDEA #49

Scoop-It Up Relay   Grades K-5

Concentration and coordination is the secret to winning this game.

Object Of The Game: To be the first team to transfer all of their candy from one container to another.

Holiday Variation: Use holiday candy (M&M's or candy corn).

Supply List

Large Spoons—one for each team
Small Candy —one for each team
Containers—2 for each team
Chairs—4

Advance Preparations:
On the day of the party:
▶ Set up two chairs for each team at opposite ends of the room.
▶ Pour the candy into two containers and place on the chairs at the far end of the room. Place the 2 empty containers on the other 2 chairs.

How To Play:
1. Divide the children into two teams. Have them line up behind the two chairs with the empty containers.
2. Give the first person on each team a large spoon.
3. On the signal "GO", they will WALK to the chair at the other end of the room, scoop up some candy, and using only one hand to hold the spoon (younger children can use two hands), WALK to the other container and pour out the candy. They will then hand the spoon to the next person in line.
4. Play continues until one team has transferred all of their candy from one container to the next.

Variation:
• The team that drops the fewest pieces of candy will be the winner. If neither team drops any pieces, then the team that finishes first wins.

IDEA
#50 # Back To Back Relay   Grades K-5

Everyone must cooperate and work as a team to win this game.

Object Of The Game: To be the first team to place all of their balloons in their basket without using their hands.

Holiday Variations: Use holiday colored balloons.

Supply List

Balloons—1 for every 2 children
Trash Bags—2 large
Laundry Baskets—2

Advance Preparations:
► Blow up the balloons. Store in the large trash bags.
On the day of the party:
► Place the two laundry baskets at the far end of the room.

How To Play:
1. Divide the children into two teams. Everyone will then need to choose a partner from their own team.
2. Place the two bags of balloons at the starting line and have each team form a line behind them.
3. Explain the object of the game. Demonstrate how the two partners will stand back-to-back with the balloon between them. They are not allowed to use their hands. If the balloon drops, the pair must go back to the starting line and start over.
4. One the signal "GO", the first pair in each line will race to the laundry basket at the opposite end of the room and drop their balloon into the basket. They will then return to their team, "tag" the next pair in line, and sit down.
5. Play continues until everyone has deposited their balloons in their laundry basket.

Pass The Spider Race
Grades K-5

The idea of passing a spider through their clothes will give most of your guests the creeps.

Holiday Variation: While not as creepy, tie the yarn around a Christmas tree light bulb or Valentine key chain.

Object Of The Game: To be the first team to be tied together by the spider's web (yarn).

Supply List
Each <u>team</u> will need:
    Yarn—20-40 feet long
    Plastic Spider—1 large

Advance Preparations:
▶ Estimate how long the pieces of yarn should be. It must be long enough to go through both sleeves of each person on the team, and will vary depending on the number of children you will have on each team. The most important thing is to make it plenty long.
▶ Cut the yarn.
▶ Tie a piece of yarn securely to each plastic spider. Use tape if necessary.
▶ Roll the yarn into a small ball behind the spider.

How To Play:
1. Divide the children into two or more groups and have them stand in a straight line.
2. Explain the object of the game, and then demonstrate how each person will have to pass the spider up one sleeve and out their other sleeve.
3. Place the ball of yarn on the ground next to the first person in each line, and hand them the spider.
4. On the signal "GO", the first person on each team will pass the spider up one sleeve, across their chest, down their other sleeve, and out to the next person, pulling the string along as they go.
5. The first team to be all tied together wins.

IDEA #52 Marshmallow Race   Grades 2-5

This is a really fun race that is a lot more difficult than it sounds.

Object Of The Game: To be the first team to eat 6 marshmallows.

Supply List

Marshmallows—large
Bowls—small
Trash Bags—new

How To Play:

1. First have the children wash their hands.
2. Divide the children into teams of two.
3. Give each child a new trash bag.
4. Have each team lay their trash bags on the floor or ground so that the short ends (top or bottom) are touching each other. Do not stand on them. Tell them to stand at opposite ends of the trash bags.
5. Give each child a bowl with 10 marshmallows in it.
6. Tell the children to kneel on the edge of the trash bags. Everyone should be about the same distance from their teammate.
7. Explain the object of the game. Demonstrate how they must keep their hands behind their back when catching the marshmallows.
8. On the signal "GO" each child will try to toss the marshmallows into their teammate's mouth. They can NOT use their hands to help catch the marshmallows. After a marshmallow is caught, they must eat it.
9. The first team to eat 6 marshmallows wins.

Variation:

- Use small marshmallows and have the teams sit closer together.

Magical Stick Relay Grades 2-5

This balloon race takes a lot of concentration and coordination to win.

Object Of The Game: To be the first team to get their balloon completely around the course.

Holiday Variations: Use holiday colored balloons.

Supply List

Each <u>team</u> will need:
   2 **Balloons**
   2 **Sticks** (rulers, chopsticks, paper towel tubes)
   2 **Chairs**

Advance Preparations:
On the day of the party:
▶ Place the chairs at the far end of the room. These will be the turnaround points.
▶ Blow up the balloons. Each team will need one balloon.

How To Play:
1. Divide the children into two teams and line them up in straight lines.
2. On the signal "GO", the first player on each team will hold the balloon between the two sticks and quickly WALK around the chair and back to the front of the line.
3. The balloon and sticks are then handed off to the next person in line without touching the balloon. If a balloon is dropped, the player who dropped it must use the sticks to pick it up.
4. The team that finishes first wins.

IDEA
#54

Pass The Teddy Bear Grades K-5

Children of all ages will enjoy playing this fast paced relay game over and over again.

Object Of The Game: To be the first team to get the Teddy Bear back to the leader.

Holiday Variations: For Christmas use a snowman or Santa Clause, for Halloween use a plastic pumpkin and for Valentines day use a soft stuffed heart.

Supply List

Teddy Bear — one for each team

How To Play:
1. Divide the children into teams.
2. Pick one leader for each team.
3. Have the players line up behind their team leader.
4. Explain the object of the game. Demonstrate how the Teddy Bear will be passed down the row (see below). An important rule is that all the players must stay in line.
5. On the signal "Go", each team will pass the Teddy Bear down the row and back to the leader.
6. The first team to finish wins the relay.
7. Keep a running tally of which team wins and play again, but this time pass the Teddy Bear a different way.

Ways To Pass The Teddy Bear :
1. Over the head.
2. Through the legs.
3. Back to back.
4. Elbows only.
5. One handed.
6. Sitting on the floor facing forward.
7. Over the first player, through the legs of the second player, over the third player, etc.

Siamese Twin Relay   Grades 2-5

Have you ever wondered what it would be like to be a Siamese Twin? This game 'sticks' two children together and the results are quite amusing!

Object Of The Game: To be the first team to retrieve all of the objects from their bucket.

Holiday Variations: Use holiday colored buckets and holiday appropriate prizes.

Supply List

2 **Buckets**
1 **Prize** for each guest (key chains, erasers, balls, pencils, pins, magnets, etc.)
2 **Chairs**
Masking Tape

Advance Preparations:
On the day of the party:
▶ With the masking tape, mark the two starting lines. Place the chairs at the opposite end of the room.
▶ Divide the prizes evenly and put in the buckets.
▶ Place the buckets on the chairs.

How To Play:
1. Divide the children into two teams.
2. The Siamese Twins are formed by having two players stand back-to-back while linking their arms at the elbows. Have children demonstrate before the race begins. **Their arms must stay linked at all times!** Have them try to walk together. The easiest way to walk straight is to have one player walk forward while his/her partner walks backwards.
3. Have the children pair up with someone on their team. This will be their 'Siamese Twin'.
4. Have the teams form two lines behind the starting line.

5. On the signal "GO", the first set of 'Siamese Twins' will walk to the bucket.
6. When they reach the bucket, **each player** will take one prize out of the bucket and then return to the starting line. **Their arms must remain linked at all times.**
7. As soon as the first set crosses the starting line, the second set of 'Siamese Twins' should head for the bucket.
8. Continue playing until all of the children have retrieved a prize from the bucket.
9. The first team to finish wins.

Suggestions:

- Be sure to allow plenty of time for this race. It is not as easy as it may seem.
- Children often like to play this game a number of times. They get better at working together each time they play.
- Encourage the children to find a "Twin" that is their same height.
- Because of the amount of coordination that is required to play this game, it is suggested that young children not participate in this relay.

Helpful Hint

Have all the children practice walking with their twin before the race begins. The results are hilarious and a lot of fun!

IDEA #56 Sucker Relay   Grades 2-5

Children really enjoy the mystery associated with this simple game. The sucker will tell each child what they must do.

Object Of The Game: Race to one end of the room, pick a sucker and return to the line while following the instruction written on the sucker. The first team to finish the race wins.

Holiday Variations: Use small boxes wrapped in holiday paper instead of the suckers. Put instructions in each box.

Supply List

Suckers—1 for each child
Chairs—1 for each team
Holiday Sacks—1 for each team

Paper, Scissors, Tape

Advance Preparations:

▶ Think of some things to do, such as jump, crawl, hop, skip, (front wards or backwards) etc. Write the activities on a small strip of paper and tape to the stick of each sucker. Make sure each team has the same activities and store in the holiday sacks.

On the day of the party:

▶ Place the chairs at the far end of the room and put a sack of suckers on each chair.

How To Play:

1. Divide the children into teams and line them up in straight lines.
2. On the signal "GO", the first player on each team runs to the chair and picks a sucker from the sack. After reading the activity, the player goes back to their line while following the instruction on the sucker (crawls, skips, jumps, etc.) and tags the next person in line.
3. Play continues until everyone has had a turn.
4. The team that finishes first wins. Let the children keep their suckers as a prize.

Dress-Up Relay   Grades K-5

No matter what their ages, all children enjoy participating in this relay game.

Object Of The Game: To be the first team to have all of their members dress and undress.

Holiday Variations: Use formal clothes like dresses & suits for Valentines Day parties, winter clothes like coats, gloves, hats, socks and boots for Winter parties, and swim masks, towel, swim suit, bucket and pail and flip flops or sandals for spring/summer parties.

Supply List

2 Clothes Baskets
2 complete outfits of **Clothing**-as many pieces as possible

---

Advance Preparations:

▶ Gather together two sets of clothing and place in the clothes baskets. Examples of items that work well include adult hats, sun glasses, boots, coats, shirts, pants, gloves and accessories. Make sure each team has the same outfits. The more items the better.
On the day of the party:
▶ Place the two clothes baskets at the far end of the room.

How To Play:

1. Divide the children into two teams. Have the children form two straight lines across the room from the clothes baskets.
2. Explain the object of the game.
3. On the signal "GO", the first person in each line will go to the clothes basket, put on all of the clothing items and race back to their team. The clothes are then removed and passed onto the next person in line. The second person dresses in the clothes, runs to the clothes basket, removes the clothes, runs back to their team and tags the next person in line.
4. This clothing exchange continues until each child has had a turn.
5. The first team to finish wins.

Pass The Kiss Relay   Grades K-5

This simple game provides lots of fun and excitement for children of all ages.

Object Of The Game: To be the first team to unwrap all of their candy.

Holiday Variations: Use holiday wrapped Hershey® Kisses™.

Supply List

Holiday Wrapped Candy (like Hershey® Kisses™)
Gloves—2 pairs of adult
Holiday Containers—2

Advance Preparations:
► Divide the candy in half and place in the holiday containers. Have extra candy on hand in case the children want to play this game again.

How To Play:
1. Divide the children into two teams.
2. Have the teams sit in a straight line, one behind the other, on the floor.
3. Give the first person in each line the container with the candy and a pair of gloves.
4. On the signal "GO", the first person on each team will put on the gloves and unwrap one piece of candy.
5. When they are done, they will quickly remove the gloves and pass the candy container and gloves to the next person in line.
6. The game continues until everyone has unwrapped a piece of candy.

Suggestion:
• Use small mittens or gloves for younger children and oversized work gloves for older children.

IDEA #59 Pass It Fast Relay   Grades K-5

You never know what is coming next in this fast paced game.

Object Of The Game: To be the first team to pass all of the objects down their line and back.

Holiday Variations: Use holiday appropriate objects.

Supply List
Each <u>team</u> will need the following objects (just suggestions):

Balloon	**Stuffed Animal**
Slime or Gooey Putty	**Artificial Flower**
Ring	**Sticker** (back peeled off)
Cup –with water in it	**Gummy Worm**
Chair	**Holiday Container**

Advance Preparations:
On the day of the party:
▶ Set up two chairs at the far end of the room.
▶ Place one of each item in the container.

How To Play:
1. Divide the children into two teams. Have them form two lines.
2. Position one adult at the front of each line. They will be in charge of passing out the objects and telling the children when it is okay for the next item to be passed. (Pass the sticker last.)
3. On the signal "GO", the first child in each line is handed an object. It is passed down the line until it reaches the chair. As soon as the object is placed on the chair, the next item is started.
4. When all the objects are on the chair, the last person in line begins passing them back, one at a time.
5. The first team to finish wins.

Variation:
• Have the children sit on the floor with their legs crossed and all facing the same direction. They must pass the objects over their heads without turning around. This really takes team work.

IDEA #60 Balloon Platter Relay

Grades K-5

The balloons seem to have a mind of their own for this relay.

Object Of The Game: To be the first team to race around the chair and back while keeping the balloons on their plate.

Holiday Variations: Use holiday colored balloons and paper plates. For Halloween draw faces on white balloons for a "ghostly platter relay".

Supply List

Balloons—1 for each child	**Trash Bags**—2 large
Paper Plates—1 for each child	**Chairs**—2

Advance Preparations:
▶ Blow up the balloons. Store in the large trash bags.
On the day of the party:
▶ Place the 2 chairs at the opposite end of the room.

How To Play:
1. Give each child a balloon and a paper plate.
2. Divide the children into two teams and line them up in straight lines.
3. Explain the object of the game and demonstrate. If the balloon falls off of the plate, they must STOP, pick it up, put it back on the plate and continue.
4. On the signal "GO", the first person in each line will place their balloon on their plate, race around a chair and tag the next person in line.
5. Play continues until everyone has had a turn.

Variation:
• To make this game more difficult, make them go back to the starting line if they drop their balloon.

IDEA #61 **Mysterious Relay**   Grades 2-5

The special directions in each balloon puts a frenzied twist into this noisy relay.

Object Of The Game: To be the first team to complete all the activities in their balloons.

Holiday Variations: Use holiday colored balloons.

Supply List

Balloons—1 for each child
Paper—2 pieces
Trash Bags—2 large

Advance Preparations:

▶ Cut the piece of paper into small pieces (about 3"x ½").

▶ Think of some 'activity' (crawl under a table, rock in the rocking chair, eat some crackers and whistle, run up the stairs, sing "Twinkle Twinkle Little Star", etc.) and write it on two of the little pieces of paper. Place these slips of paper in separate stacks (1 stack for each team). Continue writing activities until you have one for each child.

▶ Using one stack of activities at a time, roll up each slip of paper and put it into a balloon. Carefully blow up the balloons (hold the balloon downward so the paper stays away from the blowing end). Store in the large trash bags. Repeat with the second stack.

On the day of the party:
▶ Place the two bags of balloons at the opposite end of the room.

How To Play:
1. Divide the children into 2 teams and line them up in straight lines.
2. Explain the object of the game and tell them they most pop a balloon and do the 'activity' inside it before returning to their line.
3. On the signal "GO", the first person in each line will run to the bag, pick a balloon, pop it, read the activity, do the activity and finally, tag the next person in line.
4. Play continues until everyone has had a turn.

Almost A Kiss Relay
IDEA #62

Grades K-5

This friendly game is fun to watch because no one wants to get too close to the person they are passing the candy to.

Object Of The Game: To be the first team to pass the ring from person to person without using their hands.

Holiday Variations: Use Holiday colored straws and rings.

Supply List

Drinking Straws—1 for each child
Small Rings—1 for each team and extra for prizes

How To Play:

1. Divide the children into two teams. Have the children form two straight lines.
2. Pass out one straw to each child.
3. Explain the object of the game and demonstrate how they will be allowed to pass their ring. If the ring should drop on the floor, the person who dropped it needs to pick it up without using his/her hands. (This can be hard and hilarious!)
4. The first two children in each line will put their straws in their mouths and a ring is placed on the straw of the first player.
5. On the signal "GO", the first child will turn around and place the ring on the straw of the next player without using their hands.
6. The game continues until the ring has been passed all the way to the end of the line.
7. Award everyone a ring just for playing the game.

Variations:

- Let younger children use their hands to steady their straws and to pick up the ring if it falls on the floor.
- Other items that are fun to pass around include pretzels and candies that have holes in the middle (make sure the straw can easily fit through the hole.
- Cut the straws shorter if the children are having trouble controlling their straws.

IDEA #63

Soaking Wet Relay   Grades K-5

Yes you will get wet with this exciting relay race. Before playing, make sure everyone doesn't mind getting wet.

Object Of The Game: To be the first team to fill their bucket with water.

Supply List

Buckets—2 for each team
Large Sponge—1 for each team
Water

How To Play:

1. Divide the children into 2 teams and line them up in straight lines.
2. Place the bucket filled with water at the front of each line and the empty bucket behind the last person in each line.
3. Explain the object of the game.
4. On the signal "GO", the first person in each line dunks the sponge into the water and then quickly passes it over their head and to the next person in line. The sponge will continue to be passed over their heads from one child to the next until it reaches the last person in line.
5. The last person will squeeze all of the water (at least what is left) into the empty bucket and then run to the front of the line. They will then dunk the sponge into the water bucket and give it to their team who will again pass the sponge over their heads to the end of the line.
6. The first team to completely fill up their bucket with water wins.

Variations:

- Use a smaller bucket at the end of the line.
- Set a time limit.
- Spread out the lines so there are a couple feet between each team member, and have them throw the sponge to each other.

IDEA #64 Wheelbarrow Race Grades K-5

Children enjoy loading up their wheelbarrows and then racing to the finish line. It sounds easy, but it can be tricky.

Object Of The Game: To be the first team to get their loaded wheelbarrow across the finish line.

Supply List

Wheelbarrow—1 for each team
Blocks, Stuffed Animals, Balls, Trucks, Dolls, etc.— Each team must have similar items

---

Advance Preparations:
On the day of the party:
▶ Place the different items around the yard. Make sure all the items for one team are in one area, and not too close to the other team's area.

How To Play:
1. Divide the children into two teams.
2. Tell them the object of the game.
3. As a team, they will work together to push their wheelbarrow across the lawn, loading it up with items (blocks, toys, trucks, balls, etc.) as they go and then make it back across the finish line. Team members can not race ahead and pick up items and bring them back to the wheelbarrow. The wheelbarrow must go to each item.
4. The team that finishes first wins.

Variations:
• Blindfold the person steering the wheelbarrow and make their team members tell them where to go. This is hilarious to watch. Do not try this with young children.
• Use small plastic wheelbarrows for young children.
• Run as a relay race, where each team member must push the wheelbarrow, retrieve an item and then come back and unload it before the next person in line can go.

Dot Race

Grades K-5

There can be a lot of strategy to this game...each player must decide how far away they should place their dot.

Object Of The Game: To be the first person to cross the finish line.

<hr>

Supply List

Construction Paper—2 sheets for each child
Scissors
Candy "DOTS" —for prizes

<hr>

Advance Preparations:
▶ Cut the pieces of construction paper into big round dots. They must be large enough for the children to stand on.

How To Play:
1. Have the children line up in a straight line next to each other.
2. Give each child two dots.
3. Tell them to stand on one of their dots (dot #1).
4. Explain the object of the game. The only way they can cross the finish line is by staying on their own dots.
5. On the signal "GO", everyone will place the dot they are holding (dot #2) on the ground in front of them. Now they must step onto dot #2 and turn around and pick up dot #1. Next they will place dot #1 on the ground in front of them. They will continue to pick-up and lay down their dots until they have crossed the finish line. They must stay on their dots at all times.
6. The first person to cross the finish line wins. Award each player a box of DOTS as they finish.

Variation:
• Run as a relay race. Divide into teams and take turns moving their dots across the finish line. Once the first team member crosses the line, the next player in line can go.

IDEA #66

Buried Treasure Dig Grades 1-5

One fun way to end a party is to let the children "dig" for their take-home party favors.

Object Of The Game: To locate the buried treasure while blindfolded.

Holiday Variations: Use holiday themed prizes.

Supply List

Large Tub <u>or</u> **Plastic Swimming Pool**
Rice <u>or</u> **Sand**
Blindfold
Party Bags
Party Favors—small wrapped toys and
    wrapped candy

Advance Preparations:

► Place the container close to the area where the children will be "digging". (When full it will be very heavy!)
► Place some of the party favors in the bottom of the tub or swimming pool. Pour the rice or sand over the party favors until covered. Add another group of party favors and cover with additional rice or sand. Continue layering party favors and rice or sand until the container is full.

How To Play:

1. Place a blindfold over the child's eyes.
2. Guide them to the container and have them kneel next to it.
3. With their hands, the child will "dig" through the rice or sand until they find a "Treasure".
4. Repeat steps 1-3 until all of the "Treasures" have been found.

Suggestion:

• Check with your local grocery or wholesale club for huge bags (50 lb.) of rice. It is fairly inexpensive and tends to be cleaner than sand.

(IDEA #67) **Dice Twister**   Grades K-5

Get ready to stretch your limbs and test your balance with his fun variation of the classic game Twister.

Object Of The Game: To be the last person standing.

> ## Supply List
> **Plastic Tablecloth**
> **Permanent Markers**—4 different colors
> **Dice**—larger the better
> **Tape**

Advance Preparations:
▶ With the markers, draw the game board on the tablecloth. It should look like the pattern in Figure 18, with each row of 6 circles being a different color.
▶ Place a piece of tape on each side of 2 dice.
▶ With the markers, draw a circle, each a different color on four sides of the dice. Mark the remaining two sides with a W.
▶ One the second dice, write RH, LH, RF, LF, W and W.

How To Play:
1. Lay the tablecloth out on the floor.
2. Have the children take off their shoes.
3. Choose one child will be the "roller" (the person who rolls the dice) and let two children play the game.
4. Two players at a time line up on opposite sides of the tablecloth.
5. The "roller" rolls the dice and tells the players which limb (RH=right hand, LH=left hand, RF=right foot, LF=left foot) to put on the rolled color. For example "Right Hand—Blue". W=Wild and the "roller" can name any limb or color that they want to.
6. Now the players must follow the directions of the "roller". (Place their right hand on a vacant blue circle). Once a limb is placed on a circle, it can not be moved until instructed by the roller.
7. Once everyone has made the correct move, the "roller" will call out a new instruction and the players must follow the instruction.
8. The game continues until one player FALLS or lets an ELBOW or KNEE touch the tablecloth.

Figure 18
Dot Twister Game Board

Bee Swat Race   Grades K-5

This is a hilarious game to watch, and to play!

Object Of The Game: To be the first to "swat" their bee into a bucket.

> ## Supply List
> **Balloons**—yellow (at least 2 for each child)
> **Curling Ribbon**—black
> **Bucket**
> **Flyswatters**
> **Black Permanent Marker**
> **Trash Bag**—large

Advance Preparations:

▶ Blow up the balloons.

▶ With the permanent marker, draw rings around the back half of each balloon and then add two eyes and a month to the opposite end. They should resemble bumble bees.

▶ Tie an 18-inch piece of curling ribbon to the "tail" of each balloon.

▶ Store in the large trash bag.

How To Play:

1. Place the bucket on its side a good distance from the starting line.
2. Give each child a flyswatter and a balloon.
3. Have the children line up behind a starting line.
4. Explain the object of the game. An important rule is that they can only "Swat" their own balloon.
5. On the signal "Go" their children will "Swat" their bee's towards the bucket.
6. The first child to get their bee in the bucket wins.

Variation:

• Make this a relay by dividing the children into teams and then have the players take turns hitting their Bee into the bucket with a flyswatter.

• To make the game a little harder, set the bucket upright.

IDEA #69 **Candy Drop Race** Grades K-5

If the children are getting too rowdy, calm them down by playing this easy game.

Object Of The Game: To be the first person to get all of their candy into their cup.

Holiday Variation: Use holiday colored **M&M's**® or heart shaped candies for Valentines Day.

Supply List
Paper Cup—small
Napkins—small
Straws
Plastic Bag—small zip-top
Small Candies—like M&M's™ or Skittles™

Advance Preparations:
▶ Place one paper cup, one straw, one napkin and 20 pieces of candy in each plastic bag. Each child will get their own bag.

How To Play:
1. Give each child one bag.
2. Have each child take out their napkin, unfold it, and empty the contents of their bag onto it.
3. Instruct the children to place the straws on top of a piece of candy, suck in through the straw, pick up the piece of candy and place it in their cup. They can NOT use their hands, only their straws.
4. Allow them to practice this skill for a few minutes before starting the game.
5. One the signal "GO", the children will race to see who can get all of their candy into their cup first.

Suggestions:
• Younger children will have trouble sucking through a long straw, so cut the straws in half for them.

Mummy Wrap Game Grades K-5

Here is a game the children will really get wrapped up in.
Team work is the secret to success in this game.

Object Of The Game: To be the first team to wrap the mummy up so that no skin or clothing shows.

Supply List

Toilet Paper
Tape
Trash Bag

How To Play:

1. Divide the children into teams of 4-5 people.
2. Each team will pick one person to be the Mummy. The other team members will be the wrappers.
3. Give each team 3-4 rolls of toilet paper and a roll of tape.
4. Tell the children that they are to completely wrap their Mummy from head to toe so that no clothing or skin shows, except for their Mummy's nose and mouth. These cannot be covered.
5. If the toilet paper breaks, they must repair it with tape. They are trying to wrap their Mummy with one continuous roll of toilet paper.
6. Go!
7. The team that finishes first wins.

Variation:

- For younger children let them use more than 1 roll of toilet paper at a time to wrap their Mummy in.

Helpful Hint

Breaking out of the toilet paper is great fun, but really messy. A fun second game is to see which team can "trash" their mummy wrap first by putting the toilet paper in their trash bag.

(IDEA #71) Party Scavenger Hunt Grades 2-6

All of the children will enjoy searching high and low for these special items.

Object Of The Game: To find an object who's name BEGINS with each letter in the chosen phrase. Bonus points are given to the team that finds the smallest object for each letter.

Holiday Variation: Use holiday phrases like: Let It Snow; Autumn Festival; Haunting Ghosts; or Be My Valentine.

> ### Supply List
> **Paper**
> **Pencil**
> **Container**
> ___
> **Notebook Paper** (Score Pad)

Advance Preparations:
▶ Write the words BIRTHDAY PARTY (choose any phrase that you want) down the left hand side of each piece of paper. Place an X after the second occurrences of the letters R, T, A and Y since these are duplicate letters. This will be the scavenger hunt list.

How To Play:
1. Divide the children into groups of four and have them sit together.
2. Give each team a scavenger hunt list, a pencil, and a container.
3. Explain the object of the game. As they find an item, they need to write its name next to the proper letter and put it in their container. They will have 10 minutes to find as many objects as possible.
4. On the signal "GO", each team will begin to search the room for objects that begin with the letters on their scavenger hunt list.
5. When the time is up, have everyone sit down with their group.
6. Starting with the first letter on the list, 'B', have each team hold up the item they found that begins with 'B'. Give each team 1 point if they found an item that began with that letter. Award the team with the smallest item 2 extra points. Continue awarding points for each letter in the phrase.
7. The team with the most points wins.

IDEA #72 **Balloon Stuff Game** Grades K-5

*It is fun to watch your guests work as a team to win this race.
The end of this game is as much fun as the game itself.*

Object Of The Game: To stuff as many balloons into each sweat suit as possible in one minute.

Holiday Variation: Use holiday colored balloons.

> ## Supply List
> **Balloons**—small (20-30 per team)
> **Trash Bag**
> **Sweat Shirt**—extra large (1 per team)
> **Sweat Pants**—extra large (1 per team)
> **Toothpicks**
> **Stopwatch** or **Watch** with a second hand

Advance Preparations:
▶ Blow up the balloons and place half in each large trash bag.

How To Play:
1. Divide the children into two groups.
2. Have the smallest person in each group put on the sweat shirt and pants over their clothes.
3. On the signal "GO", the team members will begin to stuff the balloons into the sweat suit.
4. After one minute, shout "STOP" and the children will stop stuffing the balloons. The team with the fewest balloons left wins.
5. If time permits, play again by carefully removing the balloons and putting them back in the trash bag. Count to make sure each team has an equal number of balloons. Choose another member of the team to 'Get Stuffed'.
6. After the last game has been played, determine the winner by counting the number of balloons that have been stuffed in the sweat suit. A fun way to do this is to hand out toothpicks to all of the 'Stuffers'. The children will take turns popping the balloons with their toothpicks, one team at a time. Everyone can help count the pops!

108

(IDEA #73) # Hit The Target

This game of skill is a lot of fun on a hot summer day. ~~Small~~
water guns make good prizes for this game.

Object Of The Game: To hit as many targets as you can in
one minute.

Supply List

Balloons—different sizes
Pennies
String
Rope
Water Gun—large
Water

Notebook Paper (Score Pad), **Stopwatch** or
Watch with a second hand

Advance Preparations:

▶ Insert two pennies into each balloon and blow up.
▶ Tie different lengths of strings to the balloons.
▶ Run a rope between two trees and tie the balloons to the rope.
▶ Arrange for a place (faucet or hose) where the water gun can be
filled.

How To Play:

1. Explain the object of the game.
2. Let the children take turns shooting at the targets for one minute. When the time is up, write down the number of targets
that were hit.
3. The child that hits the most targets wins. If there is a tie, have
a 30 second "shoot-out" to determine a winner.

Variations:

• Set up different types of object: pots, buckets, shovel stuck in
the ground, stake, artificial flowers, etc. to shoot at.
• Draw faces or targets on the balloons with permanent markers.
• Hang the balloons from different trees.

IDEA #74 ## Suspended Apple Race Grades 1-5

It is quite a sight to watch children try to take a bite out of an apple that is suspended from a clothesline...it is also very difficult.

Object Of The Game: To see who can be the first to take a bite out of their apple.

Holiday Variation: Use pink (cherry flavored) bagels instead of apples for Christmas or Valentine Days parties. Just tie them to the end of the string.

Supply List
Apples—small
String
Paper Sacks—large
Clothesline or **Heavy Rope**
Needle—very large

Advance Preparations:
▶ Cut the string into 3-4 foot lengths—one for each child. The actual length will depend upon how tall the children are and whether you will be suspending the apples from a clothesline or the ceiling.
▶ With the large needle and string, thread the string through the core of the apple and then back through the other side of the apple. See Figure 19. If your apples have stems and they seem to be secure, you can tie the strings onto them. There is a good chance the stems could fall off, so I recommend threading the string through the apple.
▶ Wrap the string around each apple so that it will not get tangled up with the other apples. Store in the paper sacks.
On the day of the party:
▶ Hang the clothesline across the room.
▶ Tie some of the apples to the clothesline. Because of the various heights of children, hang some of the apples lower than others. The strings can always be shortened by tying a knot in them.

How To Play:

1. Divide the children into groups.
2. One group at a time, have each child stand by an apple that is about shoulder high. Adjust the length of the string if necessary.
3. Explain the object of the game. One very important rule is that no one can use their hands, elbows, or shoulders to help hold the apple in place.
4. On the signal "GO", the children will try to take a bite out of their apple.
5. The game is over when someone has taken a bite.
6. Give each guest the apple that they have been trying to bite.
7. Hang a new group of apples and continue playing until all of the children have had a turn.
8. If time allows, have a 'Grand Champion' race among the winners of each game.

Suggestion:

*   Have on hand an apple corer and a knife so that an adult can cut up the children's apples.
*   Have some caramel or fruit dip available for the children to dip their apples in.

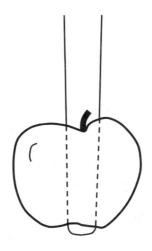

Figure 19
How to suspend an apple by a string

Party Bingo

Grades 2-5

Children of all ages enjoy this game, and because of all the variations, they never seem to get tired of it.

Object Of The Game: To be the first player to get BINGO!

Holiday Variations: Use small holiday colored candies.

Supply List

Bingo Game
Candy—like M&M's™ or Skittles™
Paper Cups—small
Wrapped Prizes or **Treats**

Advance Preparations:
On the day of the party:
▶ Pour the small candies into the paper cups. These will serve as the pieces the children will use to cover up their numbers.
▶ Set the prizes out on the table so the children can see what they might win.

How To Play:
1. Give each child a Bingo card and cup filled with candy.
2. Tell them what type of Bingo they will be playing and that the candies are to be used as markers on their cards. **DO NOT** eat the candies now, save them until the game is finished.
3. Call out the numbers until some calls "BINGO!". Check to make sure they are correct and let them choose a prize.
4. Continue playing until all of the prizes are gone.

Different Types Of "BINGO!":
- **Straight Bingo**—Any 5 numbers in a row.
- **B's & O's Bingo**—Fill in the B row *and* the O row.
- **X Bingo**—Fill in the card like the letter X.
- **Plus Bingo**—Fill in the card like a + sign.
- **Frame Bingo**—Fill in the card like a picture frame.
- **Black Out Bingo**—The whole card must be filled in.

B	I	N	G	O
●	●	●	●	●

Straight Bingo
Any 5 in a row

B	I	N	G	O
●				●
●				●
●				●
●				●
●				●

B's & O's Bingo
Fill in B and O Rows

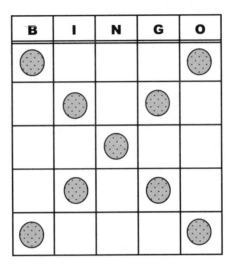

X Bingo
Fill in like the letter X

B	I	N	G	O
		●		
		●		
●	●	●	●	●
		●		
		●		

Plus Bingo
Fill in like a + sign

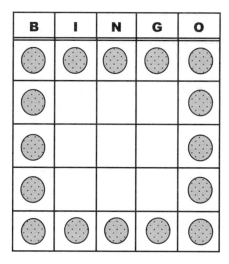

Frame Bingo
Fill in like a picture frame

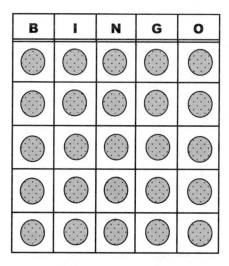

Black Out Bingo
The whole card must be filled it

Treats and Food Ideas

The treat and food ideas in this chapter are not original...in fact you have probably seen many of them before. But when it comes time to plan your party, would you have remembered them? My goal is to give you ideas for treats that are easy to make and are made out of ingredients that most children like.

Helpful Suggestions:

- Don't make too much food. Often children are not hungry because of the excitement of the party.
- Go easy on the sweet stuff. Consider serving snacks and treats that are not loaded with sugar.
- Consider letting the children make their own snacks or treats. Many of the ideas in this chapter are designed to have the children make themselves. This can be one more fun activity that you can work into your party plan.
- Ask the children if they have any food allergies before eating their treats. Some children might be too embarrassed to speak-up unless they are asked this question directly.
- Remind the children to wash their hands before making or eating their treat.

Delightful Dippers

IDEA #76

Grades K-5

Turn the kids into "Little Dippers" and watch them enjoy this fun treat.

Supply List

Marshmallows—large
Strawberries—large
Pretzels—large stick & regular
Chocolate and/or **White Chips**
Salad Oil
Candy Sprinkles
Drinking Straws—plastic
Paper Plates—colorful
Crock Pot <u>or</u> **Fondue Pot**

2-cup Glass Measuring Cup,
Spoons, Microwave

Advance Preparations:.

▶ Pour 8 ounces of chips into the glass measuring cup, and microwave on High until shiny. Chocolate chips will take from 2 to 2½ minutes and white chocolate will take from 1 to 1½ minutes. Stir until smooth and then add 1 to 2 teaspoons of salad oil and stir until mixed.

▶ Pour into a crock pot or fondue pot to keep warm.

▶ Repeat the above steps if you are using two kinds of chips.

How To Make Them:

1. Take a straw and poke into the middle of a large marshmallow.
2. Carefully dip the marshmallow in the melted chips and then quickly sprinkle with candy sprinkles.
3. Repeat step 2 with the pretzels and strawberries.

Variation:

• Use colorful sippy straws and let the children keep them as party favors.

IDEA #77 # Spicy Snack Mix Grades K-5

This spicy snack will put some real zip into your Party.

Supply List

Corn, Rice or Wheat Cereal (or any combination) - 8 cups
Peanuts—1 cup hot and spice
Cheese Crackers—1 cup hot and spicy
Pretzels—1 cup
Taco Seasoning Mix—1.25 oz
Margarine—6 Tbsp.
Worcestershire Sauce—1 Tbsp.
Hot Pepper Sauce—1 tsp.

Roasting Pan, Spoon, Paper Towels, Airtight Container

How To Make It:

1. Preheat the oven to 250°.
2. Place the margarine in a large roasting pan and melt in the oven.
3. Stir in the taco seasoning mix, worcestershire sauce and hot pepper sauce. Add one or two additional teaspoons of hot pepper sauce if you want to really spice it up!
4. Gradually stir in the remaining ingredients.
5. Bake for 1 hour, stirring every 15 minutes.
6. Spread the mixture on paper towels to cool.
7. Store in an airtight container until ready to serve.

Variation:

♦ To make a non-spicy version of this recipe use regular peanuts and cheese crackers. Replace the hot pepper sauce and taco seasoning with: ¾ tsp. garlic powder, 1½ tsp. seasoned salt, ½ tsp. onion powder. Finally, add 1 more Tbsp. of worcestershire sauce.

IDEA #78 Bugs On A Log   Grades K-5

These healthy treats might sound unusual, but the kids will really eat-em-up.

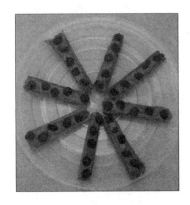

Supply List
Celery
Peanut Butter
Raisins
Mini Chocolate Chips
———
Spoon, Knife, Paper Towels

How To Make Them:
1. Wash the celery and pat dry with paper towels.
2. Cut celery into pieces (about 4-inches long).
3. With a knife, spread the peanut butter on the celery.
4. On one half of the celery sticks, press raisins randomly into the peanut butter. They should look like little bugs on a log.
5. On the remaining celery sticks, press mini chocolate chips randomly into the peanut butter.
6. They are now ready to serve.

Variations:
- Mix together peanut butter and a little honey. For the bugs, use different kinds of dried fruit.
- Instead of peanut butter, use cheese spread. For the bugs, use chopped pimientos and green or black olives.
- You could also use jalapeno cheese spread on the celery. For the bugs, use either chopped jalapenos or black olives. Most young children will not like this variation, but many adult do.

IDEA #79 Toasted Bones
Grades K-5

Children love bread sticks, so they will enjoy this fun-to-eat variation.

Supply List
Bread Sticks—refrigerated
Egg—white's only
Cinnamon Sugar

———

Small Bowl, Fork, Knife, Pastry Brush, Large Cookie Sheet, Foil

How To Make Them:
1. Preheat the oven to 350°.
2. Line the cookie sheet with foil.
3. Unroll the bread sticks and separate.
4. Roll each bread stick with your hands to make it at least 10-inches long.
5. With a knife, cut each bread stick in half.
6. At each end of the bread stick, tie a half knot. They should look like doggy chew bones.
7. In a small bowl, whisk the egg white.
8. With the pastry brush, apply a light coat of egg white to the top of each bone.
9. Sprinkle the bones with cinnamon sugar.
10. Bake for 10–12 minutes or until golden brown.

Variations:
- In addition to the cinnamon sugar topping try other toppings like Sesame Seeds, Poppy Seeds and finely grated Parmesan Cheese.

Toasted Snakes   Grades K-5

This is another creative way to use bread sticks. Boys really enjoy eating these.

Supply List

Bread Sticks—refrigerated
Egg—white's only
Cinnamon Sugar
Chocolate Chips
Peanut Butter
Fruit Tape—red
———
Small Bowl, Fork, Knife, Pastry Brush, Large Cookie Sheet, Foil, Kitchen Scissors

How To Make Them:

1. Preheat the oven to 350º.
2. Line the cookie sheet with foil.
3. Unroll the bread sticks and separate.
4. Roll each bread stick with your hands to make it at least 10-inches long.
5. At one end of the bread stick, tie a half knot. This will be the snake's head. Place on the cookie sheet and shape the rest of the bread stick in an S pattern. It should now be shaped like a snake.
6. In a small bowl, whisk the egg white.
7. With the pastry brush, apply a light coat of egg white to the top of each snake.
8. Sprinkle each snake with cinnamon sugar.
9. Bake for 10–12 minutes or until golden brown.
10. Cut the fruit tape into the shape of a snake's tongue. See the picture.
11. With a knife, cut a slit in the front of the snake's head for the mouth, and stick the tongue in it.
12. Spread the bottom of two chocolate chips with peanut butter and put in place for the snake's eyes.

(IDEA #81) **Handy Treats** Grades K-5

Children of all ages enjoy making these edible hands!
Pop extra popcorn for the children to eat while they are
making their treat.

Supply List

Popcorn
Plastic Gloves—clear
Candy Corn
Yarn—black <u>or</u> orange
Spider Rings
Plastic Cups

Scissors, Ruler, Large Mixing Bowls

Advance Preparation:
▶ Pop the popcorn.
▶ Cut the yarn into 8-inch pieces.

How To Make Them:
1. Pour the popcorn into the large mixing bowls.
2. Give each child a plastic glove, 5 pieces of candy corn, 1 piece of yarn, and a spider ring.
3. Take 5 pieces of candy corn and put in the finger tips of each plastic glove.
4. Using the plastic cups, fill each glove with popcorn. Make sure the candy corn stays in each of the finger tips while it is being filled.
5. Seal the hand by tying the yarn around the top or "wrist" of the hand.
6. Finish it off by placing the spider ring on one of the fingers.

IDEA #82 Take-Along Snack   Grades K-5

Let your child decorate the sacks and decide what snacks they want to put in them.

Supply List
Paper Sacks—any color
Stickers and Markers
Snack Foods—ideas given below
Plastic Silverware
Napkins
Stickers or **ribbon**
Plastic Bags—small zip-top

Advance Preparation:

▶ Purchase the items that you want to put in the snack bags Try to choose items that are related to your party's theme. Some possible snack foods include:

Fresh fruit	Cheese & cracker snack packs
Fruit cups	Bags of chips or crackers
Pudding cups	Fruit snacks
Jerky / meat sticks	Small bags of cookies
Juice boxes	Can of soda pop

▶ Place food in plastic bags if they are not individually wrapped.
▶ Decorate the paper sacks. You might also want to write your guests name on them.
▶ Wrap the plastic silverware in a napkin and secure with a sticker or piece of ribbon. Place in the paper sack.

How To Make Them:
1. Place all of the snack items in the paper sack.
2. Hand out to the children.

That was quick and easy!

Variation:
• Instead of paper sacks, use small to-go boxes or Chinese take-out boxes. You can usually get these from a local restaurant.

Cinnamon Tortillas   Grades K-5

This easy snack tastes great and you can let the children make it themselves.

Supply List
8 Flour Tortillas—8-inch
Sugar—2 Tablespoons
Cinnamon—1 teaspoon
Margarine—6 Tablespoons
Cookie Cutters—optional

Small Bowl, Knife, Pastry Brush, Large Baking Sheet, Paper Plates, Cutting Board

How To Make Them:
1. Preheat the oven to 400°.
2. Melt the margarine.
3. Mix the sugar and cinnamon together in a small bowl. Put in an empty salt shaker (or something similar) if you have one.
4. Lay the tortillas out on the cutting board one at a time.
5. Brush the tortillas with the melted margarine.
6. Lightly sprinkle with the cinnamon sugar mixture.
7. Cut into 8 wedges (like a pizza).
8. Spread the wedges apart on the baking sheet.
9. Bake for 4–6 minutes.
10. Enjoy!

Variation:
- Use cookie cutters that go with the theme of your party to cut the tortillas into fun shapes.

Taco Bar
Grades K-5

Every child will be able to find something good to eat at this make-your-own taco bar.

Supply List

Hamburger	Sour Cream
Taco Seasoning	Salsa
Cheese—shredded	Olives
Taco Shells	Lettuce—shredded
Tortilla Chips	

Velveeta Cheese
Diced Tomatoes with green chilies—canned

Paper Plates, Crock Pot, Fry Pan, Bowls, Spoons, Plastic Silverware, Napkins, Plastic Wrap

---

Advance Preparations:.

▶ Brown the hamburger and add the taco seasoning. Follow the directions on the package. Keep warm until party time.

▶ For a Mexican cheese sauce, place 1 lb. of Velveeta cheese and 1 can of tomatoes in the crock pot. Cook on high for about 1 hour. To speed things up, melt in the microwave first and then keep warm in the crock pot.

▶ Cook the taco shells and flour tortillas according to the directions on the packages.

▶ Place the rest of the ingredients in individual bowls and cover with plastic wrap.

How To Make Them:

▶ Set up an area where the children can make their tacos. Assemble all the ingredients on a table buffet style; plates and silverware first, followed by the taco shells and chips. Next in line will be the hamburger and the other ingredients. Put the salsa and cheese dip at the end of the taco bar.

▶ Dig In!

Fruit Pizza   Grades K-5

These individual treats can be prepared with whatever toppings each child likes.

Supply List

Cookies—large chocolate chip
   or sugar
Whipped Topping
Assorted Fruit - bananas, kiwi,
   strawberries, grapes, drained
   peach slices or pineapple

Zip-Top Plastic Bags—gallon
**Large Bowls, Large Spoons,
Paper Plates**

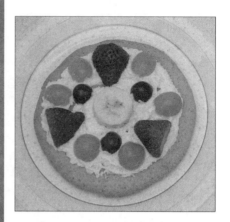

Advance Preparations:

► Bake or purchase <u>large</u> cookies.
► Thaw whipped topping.

<u>On the day of the party:</u>

► Wash and slice the fresh fruit. Store in zip-top bags. Wait to slice the bananas until the children are ready to eat.
► Drain and slice the canned fruit. Store in zip-top bags.
► Set up an area where the children will make their fruit pizzas. Place fruit in bowls. Place all of the food on a table buffet style: paper plates and cookies first, followed by the whipped topping and fruit.

How To Make Them

1. Start by placing one large spoonful of whipped topping on the cookie.
2. Add the fruit of their choice.

Variation:

• Add a drop or two of food coloring to the whipped topping for a colorful holiday variation.

Fruit Kabobs   Grades 2-5

These treats are not only fun to make, they are nutritious as well.

Supply List

Wooden Skewers
Assorted Fruit - bananas, kiwi,
   strawberries, grapes, apples,
   peaches, pineapple, melons
Marshmallows

Zip-Top Plastic Bags—gallon
Large Bowls, Paper Plates

Advance Preparations:
On the day of the party:
▶ Wash and slice the fresh fruit. Store in zip-top bags. Wait to slice the bananas until the children are ready to eat.
▶ Drain and slice the canned fruit. Store in zip-top bags.
▶ Set up an area where the children will be assembling their fruit kabobs. Start by pouring the fruit and marshmallows into separate bowls. Next, place all of the food on a table buffet style: paper plates and wooden skewers first, followed by the bowls of fruit and marshmallows.

How To Make Them:
1. Let the children put their favorite fruits and marshmallows on a skewer.

Safety Suggestion
If you are worried about the children sticking themselves with the wooden skewer, use heavy kitchen scissors to cut the sharp tips off of the skewers.

Cookie Cutter   Grades 1-5
Sandwiches   *Buy a number of different*
cookie cutters, let the children cut out their own sand-
wiches, and then give the cookie cutters to them as a take-
home party favor.

Supply List
Large Cookie Cutters—assorted
Bread
Luncheon Meats—assorted
   kinds—not thin sliced
Cheese—slices, assorted flavors
Mayonnaise
Mustard
Catsup

Knifes, Cutting Board

How To Make Them:
1. Center the cookie cutter on a piece of bread. Press down firmly until cut through. Carefully peel away the outside edges. Cut two pieces of bread for each sandwich.
2. Using the same cookie cutter, repeat step 1 with the meat and cheese of choice.
3. Next, make a sandwich from the cutout pieces by stacking them up on top of each other. Make sure you line up the edges and you add your favorite condiments.

Suggestions:
- For best results, use **large** cookie cutters that will cover almost the entire slice of bread.
- Make a variety of sandwiches. Other types that are good, especially for adults, include chicken salad, egg salad and tuna salad.
- Don't forget to have peanut butter and jelly on hand too!
- Bread that is a couple days old, yet still fresh, works the best because it won't squish down as easily.

Mini Pizzas

Grades 1-5

Let each child create their own delicious pizza...it is a guaranteed crowd pleaser.

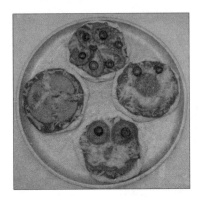

Supply List

Refrigerator Biscuits—grand size
Assorted Toppings—sausage, hamburger, pepperoni, olives, peppers, Canadian bacon, mushrooms, green peppers
Pizza Sauce
Pizza Cheese—shredded

Zip-Top Plastic Bags, Bowls, Paper Plates, Cookie Sheet, Pot Holders

Advance Preparations:
▶ Cook hamburger and sausage, cool, and place in zip-top bags.
▶ Cut-up vegetables and place in zip-top bags.

On the day of the party:
▶ Set up an area where the children will make their mini pizzas. Start by placing all the pizza toppings in separate bowls. Next, place all of the food on a table buffet style: pizza sauce first, followed by the bowls of pizza toppings. Put the cheese last in line.

How To Make Them:
1. Preheat the oven to 425°.
2. Give each child a plate with a biscuit on it. Tell them to flatten it with their hands until it makes a six-inch circle. The dough will be fairly thin.
3. Next they will go to the topping buffet and finish their pizzas.
4. Place the pizza's on a cookie sheet and bake for 10 minutes until the edges are lightly browned.

Ice Cream Sundae Party

IDEA #89

Grades K-5

It's fun to watch kids create and devour this delicious ice cream treat.

Supply List

Vanilla Ice Cream
Chocolate Syrup
Strawberry Topping
Whipped Cream Topping
Peanuts—chopped
Candy Sprinkles
Maraschino Cherries

Plastic Sundae Bowls, Plastic Spoons, Ice Cream Scoop

Advance Preparations:.

▶ Set up an area where the children can make their sundaes. Assemble all of the ingredients on a table buffet style; bowls and spoons first, followed by the ice cream and toppings. Put the whipped cream topping and cherries last.

How To Make Them:

1. Have a adult place a scoop or two of ice cream in the bowl.
2. Let the children add the ingredients for their ice cream sundae.

Variation:

• Make it a banana split party by getting rectangular bowls and adding bananas and pineapple toppings.

Helpful Hint

Go to your local ice cream shop and ask if you can buy some of their sundae bowls. Most of the time they will not charge you for them.

IDEA #90 **Spring Cupcakes**   Grades K-5

These cupcakes are super easy to make and are a great alternative to the usual cake and ice cream.

Supply List

Cake Mix	**Frosting**—white
Jelly Beans	**Gummy Worms**
Gum Drops	**Licorice**
Fruit Slice Candies	

Paper Plates, Cupcake Liners, Cupcake Baking Tin, Sharp Knife, Plastic Knives, Mixing Bowl, Mixer

Advance Preparations:.

▶ Make the cupcakes according to the directions on the box.

▶ Adults only: cut the fruit slice candies and gummy worms in half. These will be used as the antennas and wings on the butterflies.

How To Make The <u>Butterfly Cupcakes</u>:

1. Frost the cupcakes with white frosting.
2. Put a gummy worm "body" in the center of the cupcake.
3. Place 2 fruit slices on either side of the worm for the wings.
4. Finish it off by adding 2 gummy worm antennas.

How To Make The <u>Flower Cupcakes</u>:

1. Frost the cupcakes with white frosting.
2. Put the gummy worm in the bottom center of the cupcake to make the stem. Look at the picture to help with placement.
3. To make the flower, place a jelly bean or gum drop in the middle of the cupcake, then put other candies around it for the petals.
4. Finish it off by adding 2 green jelly beans on either side of the gummy worm stem for leaves.

Variations:

- Add a drop or two of food coloring to the frosting to lightly color it.
- To make a cupcake basket, just bend a piece of licorice and push it into opposite sides of the cupcake. See the picture for an example.
- Use your imagination and have fun creating different kinds of flowers and insects with bright colored candies.

<u>Did You Know?</u>

- Butterflies range in size from a tiny 1/8-inch to almost 12 inches.
- The top speed for a butterfly is 12 miles per hour.
- There are about 24,000 species of butterflies.

(IDEA #91) **Birthday Cookie**   Grades 2-5

Instead of the usual birthday cake, why not bake up one huge cookie and decorate it like you would a cake.

Supply List

Refrigerated Cookie Dough
Shortening Spray
Decorator Icing
Icing Tips
Candies/Sprinkles—optional
Baking Sheet—12-inch round

How To Make Them:

1. Grease a round baking sheet. A pizza pan works well.
2. Preheat the oven to the temperature on the cookie package.
3. Press an entire package of cookie dough onto the baking sheet. Don't worry about pressing the dough all the way to the edge of the baking sheet...just get within an inch of the edge and as the dough cooks it will expand and cover the entire baking sheet.
4. Bake according to the package directions, adding 3-4 minutes to the baking time on the package.
5. Remove from the oven. Let cool for 1 minute and then carefully loosen the cookie with a spatula. Cool completely on the baking sheet.
6. Decorate with icing and candies.

Suggestions:

- If the cookie sticks to the baking sheet after it has completely cooled, simply put it in a warm oven for a couple of minutes and it should come right off.
- Consider purchasing more than one set of tips, especially if you are using more than one color of tube icing.
- To fill in large areas like the balloons, use a large tip to put the frosting on and then use your finger dipped in water to smooth the frosting. A toothpick will also help to smooth the edges.

S'mores

Grades K-5

You probably remember making this classic treat when you were young. Go ahead and make them over a fire, or try the modern way of cooking them in the microwave.

Supply List

Marshmallows—large
Chocolate Candy Bar—plain
Graham Crackers

Small Plates, Long Handle Fork <u>or</u> **Hot Dog Stick**

How To Make Them:
Over A Campfire:

1. Take a whole graham cracker and break in half. Do the same with the chocolate candy bar. Place the candy bar on top of one of the graham cracker squares and put on a plate along with a second graham cracker square.
2. Place a marshmallow on the end of a long handle fork or hot dog stick.
3. Cook the marshmallow over a campfire until slightly browned. To help it cook evenly, turn the fork or stick while holding it over the fire. Don't get it too close to the flames or it will catch fire.
4. Place the cooked marshmallow on the chocolate and graham cracker squares, cover with the other graham cracker, squeeze the marshmallow and slowly pull the stick or fork out, leaving the marshmallow sandwiched between the graham crackers.

In A Microwave:

1. Follow the directions above, except put the marshmallow on a Styrofoam plate and cook for 8-15 seconds in a microwave. It will double in size. Stab with a fork and put between the graham crackers and candy bar.

A Real Sweet Train Grades K-5

Boys, especially will enjoy this tasty alternative to a birthday cake. Make them ahead of time, or let the children decorate their own train car.

Supply List

Swiss Cake Rolls
Chocolate Frosting
Decorator Frosting
Frosting Tips
Assorted Candies

Aluminum Foil or Waxed Paper, Large Cookie Sheet, Knife

Advance Preparations:

► Line a large cookie sheet with aluminum foil or waxed paper.
► With a fine tip and decorator frosting, draw a train track on the lined cookie sheet.

How To Make Them:

1. For the train's engine, you will need one whole and one half of a Swiss Cake Roll. Place the half roll on top of the whole roll, and line up one end of the rolls. Add candy for the wheels, front light and smoke stack. Use the chocolate frosting as glue for the candy. Finally, use the decorator frosting to draw windows on the half cake roll.
2. For the train's caboose, again you will need one whole and one half of a cake roll. This time center the half roll on top and in the middle of the whole roll. Add four candy wheels and draw on the windows like you did for the engine.
3. For the middle cars, use the chocolate frosting to glue on four candy wheels and add other candy decorations.

Variation:

• Instead of decorating with just candy, you can also use animal crackers for a circus car or pretzels for a log car. Be creative.

IDEA #94 **Leprechaun Hats** Grades K-5

These fun little cookie treats make a great addition to any St. Patrick's Day party!

Supply List

Chocolate Wafer Cookies
Hershey Kisses®
Green Decorating Icing

Small Round Frosting Tip

How To Make Them:

1. Unwrap the Hershey Kisses®.
2. With the green frosting, squeeze a dime size portion in the center of each cookie.
3. Place a Hershey Kiss® on the icing and push down until the icing comes out from around the bottom of the candy. The frosting should have formed a nice ring around it.
4. Complete the hats by drawing a small square buckle with the frosting.

Variation:

- For a Halloween party, make these into witches hats by using orange frosting.

Helpful Hint

Use a toothpick to help make the corners of the buckles square.

IDEA #95   Dirt Cups

Grades K-5

It is amazing how crushed cookies and pudding can be turned into a delightfully gross looking treat. Let the children make this treat!

Supply List

Cookies—chocolate wafer with white frosting
Chocolate Pudding
Jelly <u>or</u> **Gummy Worms**
Clear Plastic Cups

Air Tight Storage Containers, Plastic Spoons, Waxed Paper, Rolling Pin

Advance Preparations:

▶ Crush the cookies using the waxed paper and rolling pin. When you are finished, it should look like lumpy black dirt. Store in an air tight container.
▶ Prepare the chocolate pudding according to the directions on the package. Cover and refrigerate.
▶ Make a sample following the steps below. The children will get excited when they see what they are going to make.

How To Make Them

1. Begin by putting a spoonful of crushed cookies in the bottom of a plastic cup.
2. Next add a few spoonfuls of chocolate pudding.
3. Now add a worm or two.
4. Continue with another layer of cookies and pudding.
5. Top it off with a cookie layer and a couple more worms.
6. Enjoy!

Variation:

• For a girls party, make these up ahead of time and stick a pretty artificial flower in it. The worms will be a surprise!

IDEA #96

Ooey Gooey Wormy Desert

Grades K-5

Kids really enjoy "fishing" out the gummy worms in this easy-to-make dessert.

Supply List

Orange Gelatin—1 large package (8 serving size)
Water
Gummy Worms
Chocolate Sprinkles
Non-Stick Cooking Spray

Small Saucepan, Spoon, Knife, 9-inch Pie Plate

How To Make It:

1. Spray the pie plate with non-stick cooking spray.
2. Boil 1½ cups of water in a small saucepan and remove from heat.
3. Pour the gelatin into the boiling water and stir 2 minutes, or until the gelatin is completely dissolved.
4. Add 1½ cups of **cold** water to the gelatin mixture.
5. Pour the gelatin into the pie plate.
6. Refrigerate for 45 minutes.
7. Remove from the refrigerator and push the gummy worms into the thickened gelatin.
8. Refrigerate for 2 additional hours or until firm.
9. Just before serving, add the chocolate sprinkles over the top of the gelatin until it resembles dirt.
10. Garnish with additional gummy worms.

Mini Ghost Cookies Grades K-5

Children of all ages enjoy making these easy treats.

Supply List

Nutter Butter® Cookies
Vanilla Almond Bark
Mini Chocolate Chips

Small Saucepan, Large Spoon,
Tongs, Wax Paper, Cookie Sheet

How To Make Them:

1. Cover cookie sheet with wax paper.
2. Place half of the almond bark in a saucepan.
3. Melt over very low heat for 8 minutes, stirring constantly until melted and smooth. (Check the melting directions on the package of almond bark since cooking times may vary.)
4. With the tongs, carefully drop each cookie in the melted almond bark, turn until covered and then remove from the pan. Shake lightly to remove excess coating and place on the wax paper.
5. Before the almond bark hardens completely, place two mini chocolate chips on each cookie to make eyes. If you wait too long you might have to 'glue' them on with a dab of frosting.

Suggestions:

- Do NOT overheat the almond bark. Overheating can cause it to scorch or caramelize. If this happens, pour it out and start over.
- If the almond bark seems too thick for dipping, add one tablespoon or more of **solid** vegetable shortening and stir until smooth.
- Other treats that can be dipped in the almond bark include pretzels, dried fruit, marshmallows, licorice and nuts.

Variation:

- Use white frosting instead of almond bark.

Strawberry Smoothies

Grades K-5

For a healthy snack blend up a batch of these delicious smoothies. Serve them in a fun glass that the kids can take home as a party favor.

Supply List
Strawberries—frozen
Strawberry Yogurt
Orange Juice
Bananas— ripe

Blender, Large Spoon, Plastic Cups

Advance Preparations:
▶ Remove the strawberries from the freezer about 1 hour before you plan to make the smoothies.

To make 4½ cups you will need the following:
12-15 Strawberries—medium size
3 cartons of Strawberry Yogurt (6 oz.)
1 cup Orange Juice
1 ripe Banana

How To Make Them:
1. Place the partially defrosted strawberries in the blender.
2. Peel the banana, and cut into small chunks. Put in the blender.
3. Add the yogurt and orange juice to the fruit in the blender.
4. Place the cover on the blender and blend on high speed for about 1 minute or until the mixture is smooth.
5. Turn off the blender and pour into plastic cups.

Suggestions:
• Add a little crushed ice while blending to make it really cold.
• Make them ahead of time. Simply blend again before serving.
• For a creamier smoothie, use milk instead of orange juice.
• Use your favorite fruit mixed with the same flavor of yogurt.

Stencil Brownies

Grades K-5

For a fun alternative to cake and ice cream, serve these easy brownies with a fun twist.

IDEA #99

Supply List
1 **Brownie Mix** (Family Size)
1 **Baking Pan** (13"x 9")
Powdered Sugar—¼ cup
Strainer—small mesh

Bowl, Large Spoon, Scissors, Paint Brush, X-Acto Knife or Razor Blade, Paper

How To Make Them:
1. Make a copy of the snowflake patterns in Figures 20 and 21.
2. With a razor blade, carefully cut out the snowflakes.
3. Mix and bake the brownies according to the directions on the package.
4. Let them cool completely.
5. Place the paper snowflake stencils on top of the brownies. Use cut pieces of paper to cover the rest of the brownie.
6. While holding the strainer over the stencils, slowly pour some powdered sugar into the mesh strainer. Carefully tap the strainer with your hand to shake the sugar evenly over the stencils. Continue adding powdered sugar until the stencils are barely covered. Note: too much powdered sugar will make the stencil heavy and hard to pick up.
7. Carefully lift the stencils straight up and away from the brownies. It is helpful to have someone assist you with this step.
8. Use a clean paint brush to 'clean up' any powdered sugar that fell on your brownie as you removed the stencil. Dipping the brush in water will help remove the sugar.
9. Cut into pieces after your guests have arrived.

Figure 20
Snowflake Stencils

Helpful Hint:

If you use these snowflake stencils, place them on the brownies in the arrangement that you like and then cut other pieces of paper to cover the rest of the brownie. You only want the snowflakes to be white.

Figure 21
Snowflake Stencil

(IDEA #100) Snow Crunch   Grades K-5

Here is a treat that starts out as a gooey mess and ends up as a snack that is hard to resist. Kids love it!

Supply List

Cereal—like Crispix® or Corn Chex®
Margarine
Peanut Butter
Chocolate Chips
Powdered Sugar
Zip-Top Plastic Bag—gallon
Large Mixing Bowl
Large Spoons

How To Make It:

1. Start by putting the following in the sauce pan:
   - 1 stick of margarine
   - 1 cup peanut butter
   - 1 12 oz bag of Chocolate Chips
2. Pour half of a box of cereal into the large mixing bowl.
3. Cook the above ingredients over medium heat until melted. Stir continuously to keep it from scorching.
4. Pour the melted chocolate mixture over the cereal and stir until well coated. Add additional cereal if necessary.
5. Pour 1½ cups of powdered sugar into the zip-top plastic bag. Add the coated cereal, seal the bag and shake. Keep shaking until the cereal is well coated. Add additional powdered sugar if necessary.

Variation:

- For a holiday variation, use powdered food coloring to color the powdered sugar. Powdered food coloring is available online or at most cake supply stores.

IDEA #101 Snowman Cupcakes   Grades K-5

These cute cupcakes make a perfect treat for any winter-time party.

Supply List

Cake Mix
Frosting—white
Marshmallows—large
Pretzel Sticks
Chocolate Chips—mini
Chocolate Candies—assorted
Fruit Slice Candies
Fruit Leather

Paper Plates, Plastic Knifes, Cupcake Liners, Cupcake Baking Tin, Paring Knife <u>or</u> Kitchen Scissors, Mixing Bowl, Zip-Top Bags, Mixer

Advance Preparations:

▶ Make the cupcakes according to the directions on the box.
▶ Use a paring knife or kitchen scissors to cut a marshmallow into two pieces. Make one piece smaller than the other. To help cut the marshmallows, dip the knife or scissors in some water and keep it moist while cutting the marshmallows.
▶ Use the paring knife or kitchen scissors to cut the fruit leather into narrow strips. These will be used as scarves. Also cut small slices of fruit leather into the shape of a mouth.
▶ Place all the cut pieces in zip-top bags to keep them from drying out.

How To Make Them:

1. Frost the cupcakes with white frosting. Save a little frosting to use as glue for the snowmen. Set aside.

2. To make a snowman, you will stack 3 marshmallows on top of each other. The whole marshmallow is on the bottom, followed by the smallest marshmallow piece, and then the larger piece will be the head. Use some frosting to "glue" the 3 marshmallows together.

3. Make a hat out of candy. For one hat we used a thin mint topped with an M&M. For another we used a gummy lifesaver topped with a gum drop. Our third hat was a mini peanut butter cup topped by a Skittle. Two were topped by a small round chocolate ball. Use frosting to "glue" the candies together. Place your hat on top of the snowman's head.

4. Bend the fruit leather scarf around the snowman's neck and loop one end over the other. Use a little frosting to hold in place if necessary.

5. Dip the mini chocolate chips in frosting and add them to the snowman as a nose, eyes and buttons.

6. Press two pretzels into the middle marshmallow for the snowman's arms. You might need to break off one end of each pretzel if they are too long.

7. Finally, use a little frosting to "glue" the fruit leather mouth in place.

8. Place the snowman on top of a frosted cupcake.

Variation:

• Make a melting snowman by cutting the bottom marshmallow at a steep angle. The snowman to the far right in the picture is an example of what one might look like.

Suggestion:

♦ If you are going to move these cupcakes around very much (take to a school party) you will need to poke a toothpick or pretzel up through the middle of the marshmallows to help them standup.

Order Form

101 Quick & Easy Party Ideas For Kids

<u>Book Price:</u>
Each copy of *<u>101 Quick and Easy Party Ideas For Kids</u>* costs **$9.95** plus shipping and sales tax (if applicable). All orders of three or more books qualify for a discount. Call 800-757-7124 for additional volume discount information.

<u>Shipping:</u>
$2.50 for the first book and $1.00 for each additional book. Priority Mail is available for $3.85 for the first book and $0.50 for each additional book.

<u>Sales Tax:</u>
Please add $0.78 for each book shipped to Missouri addresses.

<u>Delivery Time:</u>
Please allow 1-3 weeks for delivery.

<u>Send Orders To:</u>   Creative Kids Products
9825 NE 116th St
Kansas City, MO 64157

Please send _____ copies of *<u>101 Quick and Easy Party Ideas For Kids</u>* to the following:

Name: _____

Address: _____

City: _____ State: _____ Zip: _____

I have enclosed a check or money order for $_____

Please make check or money order payable to **Creative Kids Products**

If you would like an autographed copy, simply include the name of the person that will be receiving the book.

For up-to-date information about our other titles, please visit our web site at:

FunPartyBooks.com

Our other titles include:

- ♦ 101 Spooktacular Party Ideas
- ♦ 101 Classroom Party Ideas
  (available August 2005)

Order Form
101 Quick & Easy Party Ideas For Kids

Book Price:
Each copy of _101 Quick and Easy Party Ideas For Kids_ costs **$9.95** plus shipping and sales tax (if applicable). All orders of three or more books qualify for a discount. Call 800-757-7124 for additional volume discount information.

Shipping:
$2.50 for the first book and $1.00 for each additional book. Priority Mail is available for $3.85 for the first book and $0.50 for each additional book.

Sales Tax:
Please add $0.78 for each book shipped to Missouri addresses.

Delivery Time:
Please allow 1-3 weeks for delivery.

Send Orders To: Creative Kids Products
9825 NE 116th St
Kansas City, MO 64157

Please send _____ copies of _101 Quick and Easy Party Ideas For Kids_ to the following:

Name: _____

Address: _____

City: _____ State: _____ Zip: _____

I have enclosed a check or money order for $_____

Please make check or money order payable to **Creative Kids Products**

If you would like an autographed copy, simply include the name of the person that will be receiving the book.

For up-to-date information about our other titles, please visit our web site at:

FunPartyBooks.com

Our other titles include:

- ♦ 101 Spooktacular Party Ideas
- ♦ 101 Classroom Party Ideas
      (available August 2005)